Sanborns' Camp

A Memoir

By

"Doc" Sanborn

For information address: Doc Sanborn
2001 32 Street West
Bradenton, FL 34205

ISBN-13: 978-1493754946
ISBN-10: 1493754947

Front cover illustration by Al Musitano

Manufactured in the United States

DEDICATION

This book is dedicated to Kathryn Miller, Ph.D. and our SSCF writing group. Thanks for encouraging the dream.

ACKNOWLEDGEMENTS

My appreciation to Dona Lee Gould for her unerring eye and guidance, to Al Musitano for his cogent suggestions and art work, to the members of the Manatee Writers' Group of the Florida Writers' Association for their patience and helpful criticisms, and to Gail Bicknell for her support, commentary, and inspiration.

PATRILINEAL LINE OF DONALD E SANBORN III

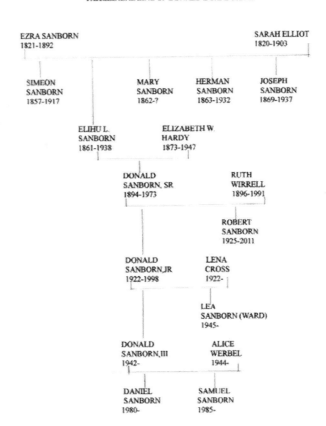

EZRA SANBORN
1821-1892

SARAH ELLIOT
1820-1903

SIMEON
SANBORN
1857-1917

MARY
SANBORN
1862-?

HERMAN
SANBORN
1863-1932

JOSEPH
SANBORN
1869-1937

ELIHU L.
SANBORN
1861-1938

ELIZABETH W.
HARDY
1873-1947

DONALD
SANBORN, SR
1894-1973

RUTH
WIRRELL
1896-1991

ROBERT
SANBORN
1925-2011

DONALD
SANBORN, JR
1922-1998

LENA
CROSS
1922-

LEA
SANBORN (WARD)
1945-

DONALD
SANBORN, III
1942-

ALICE
WERBEL
1944-

DANIEL
SANBORN
1980-

SAMUEL
SANBORN
1985-

TABLE OF CONTENTS

Dedication
Acknowledgements

1.	The Legend Begins	1
2.	The Outhouse	46
3.	The Honolulu Connection	58
4.	Mr. Irving	71
5.	Lady Slippers	80
6.	The Cove	90
7.	Repairing Road	106
8.	The Boat House	119
9.	The Waterpipe	124
10.	The Ice House	139
11.	The Rowboat	148
12.	Bloodsuckers, Blueberries, and Beach Sand	157
13.	The Patio	166
14.	Pine Branches and Privacy	171
15.	The Dock	179
16.	Sailing	183
17.	The Appendectomy	191
18.	Kayaking	198
19.	Repression	218
20.	PTSD	220
21.	Grandma and Jack and MLK and…	224
22.	The Legend Ends	236

THE LEGEND BEGINS

In May of 1880, jockey, George Lewis, rode the sleek racehorse, Fonso, to victory in the 6th Kentucky Derby. About the same time and a thousand miles north in New Hampshire, my great-great-grandfather, Ezra Sanborn, worked his horses into a lather as well, and achieved his own small victory.

"Whoa, Goliath. Whoa, Hercules." Ezra pulled back on the reins and the two huge Percherons stopped their ponderous plodding. The rattling plow ceased its noisy forward momentum. In the ensuing silence, the hum of insects was suddenly noticeable. A small clump of earth fell from the moldboard, its dropping making the barest whisper. Goliath whickered and switched his tail at an annoying, green-eyed horsefly on his rump.

Ezra looked back on the newly turned furrow-- straight as the ocean's horizon-- and grunted to himself in satisfaction. The last furrow in a large field of freshly plowed parallel rows signaled the end of that particular labor. "Yup," he murmured, "there's a right way and wrong way to do things and that there furrow's just about as right as it can get."

He unhitched the plow and led the draft horses into the barn.

"Pa?" The voice of nineteen-year old Elihu, his second-born son, startled Ezra for a moment. He turned to see him standing by Goliath's stall.

"Sorry, Pa. I didn't mean to make you jump. I

was just going out to meet you. I was hoping we could talk for a minute."

Ezra eyed the lanky frame of his son, noted the earnest look on his face, and said, "Course we can talk. Just can't stop work to do it. There's still chores to be done afore supper. So grab a bucket and help me water these critters and we'll talk on the way. You should know by now how much we got to do on this here farm."

"I do know, Pa, and that's sort of what I wanted to talk with you about."

"Oh?" Ezra passed the reins of Hercules to Elihu, who led the massive horse into his stall while Goliath went into the adjoining one. Father and son filled water buckets at the well pump outside the barn and carried them back to the stalls.

"I couldn't sleep the other night. It was hot and I was restless. I was going out on the porch for a bit. I thought it would be cooler. And as I was coming down the back stairway, I heard you and Ma talking in the kitchen."

Elihu looked down at his feet. " I didn't want to barge right in if you were talking personal like, so I stopped for a minute other side of the door. Then I heard my name mentioned, so of course I listened a bit. I wasn't really meaning to be nosey."

Ezra raised his eyebrows at this, but only said, "Go on."

"Well, you were talking about what to do with the farm when you got older, and Simeon, being the oldest son, should inherit the farm. Mom said she couldn't stand to see me hurt like that. I remember her suggestion of splitting the farm between us, but you said that was only asking for trouble, that sooner or later we'd have differences we couldn't reconcile, and then the family would get torn apart with members taking one side or another. You both seemed sad and upset about the whole thing."

Elihu shifted his weight and looked uncomfortable, but doggedly continued, "You both felt that I loved working on the place and that made the decision difficult."

"You seem to have heard quite a bit for someone not wanting to be nosey," Ezra noted dryly.

"I said I didn't mean to. I wasn't meaning to listen on purpose…well, I was…sort of, but not really. You know what I mean."

"Keep talking," was Ezra's laconic reply.

"Well, I gave a lot of thought to what you and Ma said. And I do love the farm, but it's not the farm work itself that I love. It's the fixing of things on the farm. I like working with my hands. You've taught me a lot about those kinds of things, what tools to use for what kind of job. How to have the patience to measure twice and cut once so's I don't mess up. I really liked building the wood shed and the hayrick. I liked repairing the roof when it leaked over the kitchen. And everybody likes the new outhouse I built."

Ezra interrupted "So you like making things and you don't like shoveling horse pucky. And you like building stuff and you don't like milking and planting. Is that about it?"

"Yup. That's about it, except it solves your problem about the farm. I think I want to be a carpenter. So I need to find someone I can apprentice to for a while and then go out on my own. Anyway, Simeon really should get the farm. He loves the whole thing, the animals, planting, putting stuff by, all that."

Ezra looked at his son thoughtfully. "We should talk more often. But I guess it's not in our nature 'til it's a necessity…pity."

Elihu nodded. "I never really thought it through before, my future and what I want to do with it. You know how one day kind of blends into the next. But I'm glad I did. And I'm glad you're not mad at me."

Ezra's lips twitched. "Well, this will sure put your ma at ease--and me too. So now we need to hitch you up with a master carpenter. There's old Mr. McKutchin in town. Most folks have used him at one time or another. He's getting along in years and probably could use a young buck like you to do the heavy lifting. His wife died a ways back and he's gotten crotchety cuz of it. The point is, he needs a helper, but he's not easy to get along with these days. If we can reach an understanding, you're going to be his slave labor for a couple years."

Elihu nodded. "I know, Pa."

Ezra continued, "Meanwhile, you can stay here and help out. When you do leave, your younger brother, Herman, isn't going to be too happy about taking on some of your chores in addition to his own. I guess we'll all be taking on a bit more."

* * *

In April 1881, Billy the Kid escaped with his life from the Lincoln County Jail in Mesilla, New Mexico. It made the news. About the same time and almost two thousand miles northeast, Elihu finally made his escape from the farm. While it represented a life-changing event for him, no one considered it newsworthy.

He worked with old man McKutchin for two years. It turned out the old man was terribly lonely and Elihu was a good listener. After a bit they developed a quasi father-son relationship. Elihu was given the back bedroom. They took meals together. Often in the evening, McKutchin would talk about times past, the inventions he'd seen come and go, and old customs and friends that faded away. Sometimes he'd talk of Mrs. McKutchin, his voice soft and quavery, how she always seemed glad to see him when he got home from work-- even when he simply entered the room, how she always tried to please him--even in silly inconsequential ways. They weren't silly in the long run. He never doubted once in those long years of marriage that she loved him and that he was her priority.

"If you ever find one like her, do whatever you can to wed her, cuz you'll never find a better wife."

"She sounds like a wonderful woman," Elihu

said earnestly.

"She was one in a million. God, how I miss her."

Those times he went to bed late, occasionally with a bottle, with shoulders slumped, eyes red-rimmed and wet. It was the mornings following such reminiscing that found him crotchety--the hangover didn't help much either. The old man's sadness caused Elihu's heart to ache and he vicariously learned the depth, dimensions, longevity, and unswerving devotion of mature love.

Old man McKutchin was a good teacher and Elihu an apt pupil. Townsfolk noticed the quality of his work. Mr. McKutchin gave him more jobs to do on his own.

One day, old man McKutchin climbed a ladder to check the trusses of a new roof they were trying to complete before the weekend. Elihu watched from the ground where he was holding the ladder steady. McKutchin bent forward to squint at a joint. He uttered a funny choking sound, grabbed his chest, and plummeted to the ground, landing head first. It sounded like a baseball bat hitting a Halloween pumpkin.

Over the next couple days, Elihu finished the roof. It seemed to be the right thing to do. Then again, he didn't know what else to do.

When it came time for the homeowner, Mr. Slive, to pay, he refused, saying his contract was with old man McKutchin and he was dead.

Elihu said hotly, "That's not right and you

know it."

"Go about your business," Slive snarled. "This doesn't concern you."

"If you don't do what's right, I'll make it everybody's business I talk to…and I talk to a lot of people in my business," Elihu threatened. (that wasn't really true, carpentry could be rather solitary, but he saw no point in enlightening Mr. Slive).

It ended with Mr. Slive giving Elihu $25.00.

Elihu missed old man McKutchin. Every time he passed Mr. Slive on the street, they glared at each other. Elihu decided it was time to move on and soon went south to Concord where there was more work.

He did well and spent little--except on books. He discovered he enjoyed reading and learning. He figured it was too late to go to college. He probably couldn't get in anyway, but there was no reason he couldn't learn stuff on his own.

He put a little money aside. He dated a few times, but found the girls simpering, boring and immature. If only he could find a girl like Mrs. McKutchin.

* * *

In March, 1888, the Great Blizzard struck the northeast, killing four hundred people and dropping close to two feet of snow in New York City. It was worse in Maine, Vermont, and New Hampshire.

Elihu received a letter from his mother, asking him to come home. The blizzard had buried the farm in mountains of snow. One particular drift between the farmhouse and the barn topped seventeen feet at the crest. Cows had to be milked and fed somehow. Simeon, Herman, Joseph and his father had spent all day shoveling a tunnel to the barn, resulting in his father having a heart attack. They couldn't get to a doctor until three days later and by the time the doctor got there, Ezra, who had spent those days in bed, was back on his feet and shuffling around, albeit slowly. Even though he survived, he was now at risk for another attack, according to the doctor. The family needed Elihu's help. And so he came back to the farm--to milking, planting, and shoveling horse and cow pucky.

Survival is not synonymous with recovery. While Ezra survived his heart attack, he never fully recovered. His drive, his stamina, and his spirit were fractured. He just wasn't the same man afterwards. Occasionally there were glimpses of the old Ezra, but they were short-lived--tortuous teases for those who wanted him back, as well as to himself. His focus shifted from prosaic practicalities to the eschatological. Where once he dauntlessly confronted any challenge farm life presented, now he readily deferred to Simeon. He was seen reading the Bible before bedtime--not his usual practice, and on more than one occasion, he was heard to mutter, "No one leaves this life alive" and "pretty soon I'm going to find out what's on the other side." Many of his sentences began with, "When I'm gone...."

The snows finally melted and pastures turned green. Farm life returned to normal under Simeon's direction--as normal as it could be with Ezra's limited labor. Elihu's help could be relinquished and he was eager to resume his vocation. He liked the Concord and nearby Hopkington area and returned there. However, he came back to the family farm frequently. His father's failing reminded him sharply of old man McKutchin and he wanted to make the most of whatever time was left.

During one visit home, Ezra told him that he'd heard the Hardies were looking for some carpentry help. They were planning to build a family fishing camp on Newfound Lake. Elihu decided he'd look into it.

*   *   *

Elihu walked up the front pathway to the Hardy home in Franklin, New Hampshire, and eyed the large but modest house before him. David Hardy had done well for himself. The house, once the family farm, was now the family homestead. The livestock were long gone, pastures sold, and an expanding village had grown up around it. The house looked attractive and lived in. Elihu squinted a trained eye at the ridgepole, looking for any sign of sag. There was none. White curtains framed the windows. Large rose bushes lined the walkway. He reached up to knock.

"Hello, Elihu." A soft voice, but firm and redolent with hidden meanings, came from his side. He whirled around to see a face embosked in a rose bush and stared at luminous, deep, brown eyes that sparkled with amusement and full lips parted in a slight smile. Curly chestnut hair framed a broad forehead and wide cheekbones and a slight smile that stopped him in his tracks. He hadn't seen her pruning the roses.

"I'm Lizzie. Dad said you'd be by sometime today. We're supposed to entertain you until he gets home from work, which should be anytime now."

Elihu stammered out a greeting, suddenly feeling light-headed and weak-kneed. He had never seen such an arresting-looking girl. She appeared much younger than he, but remarkably self-assured. He felt awkward. Looking around for someone else hidden in the bushes he said, "Who's 'we?'"

Her laughter was light and friendly, "'We' is me and my mom, and she is in the kitchen and looking forward to meeting you. Follow me."

She turned and led the way inside the house. She stopped in the living room, saying, "I'll go get her. Make yourself comfortable."

Lizzie returned a few moments later with her mother, a slender, attractive woman of indeterminate age and wearing a friendly smile.

"Hello, Elihu. I'm Sarah.

Elihu liked her smile and easy manner.

"My husband will be home any minute now.

David and I know your parents and I remember seeing you at the Fox family reunion five years ago--your mother is somehow related to the Foxes, you know--well, we're all related in one way or another--the Foxes, the Hardys, and the Sanborns--but we've never actually met you. I'm glad to finally get to know you."

Elihu, who thought the various family interrelationships to be a spider web of confusion, merely grinned, nodded and said, "It's real nice to meet you too, ma'am.

"Please, just call me, Sarah."

"Okay, Sarah."

"Would you like some cider? You must be thirsty from traveling."

As Elihu sipped a mug of cool cider, he surreptitiously studied his surroundings. The living room was large and comfortable with furniture that was worn, but not shabby. A huge fieldstone fireplace dominated the inside wall with wood neatly stacked in a storage section to the left of the firewall. A doorway to the right led to the kitchen while another door to the left showed stairs leading to the second floor. In the center of the wooden plank floor lay a large braided rug. From the corner of his eye, he picked out Lizzie, that same arresting slight smile still playing along her lips. She was looking at him with an openly appraising expression. His surveillance was abruptly curtailed by the noisy opening of the front door behind him and the appearance of a burly, bearded man of middle age, but still hale and hearty.

"David," Sarah called, "come meet Elihu. He arrived only a few minutes ago."

David Hardy strode toward him and proffered his hand. They shook, studying each other.

"So, you're Ezra's son. I hear you're a skilled carpenter and in between jobs."

"Yes, sir…to both."

"I guess you know a bit about our project or you wouldn't be here."

"I heard that you wanted to build a family fishing camp on Newfound Lake."

David grinned, "That's it in a nutshell. Are you interested?"

"I think I am, but I'd like to know more…like how big, how many rooms, what kind of foundation, how soon, what's the time frame…stuff like that."

"Well, I guess you and I have a lot to talk about. Why don't we get you a refill on that cider and go out back by the woodpile and start dickering."

* * *

In January, David Hardy, his son, Edward, Jonathan Fox, and Elihu led a team of horses pulling a sled laden with lumber and tools across the ice of Newfound Lake to a slender finger of land on Pike's Point. Come spring, they would begin building the families' fishing camp.

The hillsides around Newfound Lake were in the last stages of being denuded by the logging industry. Felled trees were dragged by oxen or horse team down to the lake shore where large rafts of these logs were floated down the lake with the prevailing northwesterly winds. At the foot of the lake, abutting a lovely sandy beach, was a saw mill, drying sheds, and ancillary structures. Board lumber was transported to the railhead in Bristol and shipped south to Franklin, Concord, and Boston. The saw mill and its vicinage was called Slab Village. When the heyday of logging ended a few years later, so did the village. The lovely sandy beach remained.

Elihu and company met at Slab Village and loaded the horse-drawn sled with the building materials needed and began the half-mile trudge to Pike's Point. As Elihu trekked beside the sled, the snow crunching under his boots, there was no way he could imagine that sixty years later, his grandson and fiancée would drive a car across the same icy route on a dark winter's night, cautiously skirting the gaping holes left by the ice harvesters. Instead, he contented himself with recollections of his burgeoning romance with Lizzie.

A week ago, Lizzie invited him to accompany her to a Chautauqua lecture in Concord where Russell H. Conwell gave his famous "Acres of Diamonds" speech, the gist of which was, "It's one's moral duty to get rich...." When it was over, she asked him what he thought of Conwell's central thesis. Since he'd spent much of the lecture eyeing her from his peripheral vision and fantasizing about their relationship, he was unprepared for her question. He hopefully offered a brief and noncommittal response, to which, she replied with an arch smile, "I know that with your intelligence and insight, you will give me a more penetrating analysis when you're ready."

Elihu didn't know if he was being pushed, pulled, or subtly inspired. He did know he was motivated to continue his pursuit.

Lizzie made it apparent early on that she was interested in him as a potential mate. However, "interested" was not the same as pledged. She was still assessing, and at times he felt like a work horse at auction, being scrutinized for strengths and weaknesses. At any moment he half-expected her to open his mouth and examine his teeth. And if she had been asked if this courtship process was in reality an inspection process, she would have freely agreed. After all, she wouldn't buy a pig in a poke.

For his part, Elihu was besotted, enthralled, totally smitten. He thought her beautiful, smart, not too pushy, skilled in wifely duties, and a wonderful deipnosophist (he hadn't minded when she taught him the definition: "an adept conversationalist at table"). He'd whiled away many an hour in daydreams about a life with her. He would marry her tomorrow, but she'd made it plain that she wasn't ready to talk about that yet. Elihu had found his Mrs. McKutchin.

"Hey, Elihu. Watch where you're going!"

David's shout startled Elihu out of his reverie. He barely missed stepping in an abandoned ice fishing hole. The realization that he had come close to breaking his leg banished all daydreams--for a while.

Arriving at David's property, they put sturdy horse blankets on the team while they cooled down. Even though the sun was shining the temperature hovered around freezing. The lumber was stacked with boards between layers to continue the drying process. The horses and men huddled in the lee of the lumber pile. The former got feed bags of oats, the latter, thick chunks of cheese and bread.

Elihu looked across the lake to the mountains north and west, then to the cove on the east. "This is one beautiful spot you have."

David looked around and nodded in assent,

"Yes, it is. I've been all over this lake fishing, and I think this is one of the prettiest." He grinned and added, " Sarah and Lizzie like it too. I brought them here last fall to look it over. Like me, they fell in love with it."

He paused, then continued with a sly smile, "If you intend to spend much time with Lizzie, you'd best like it as well."

Elihu coughed on a bread crumb. "Well, I do."

"And you do seem to be spending a lot of time with her."

"Well, I have seen her more than usual lately."

"I guess the heck you have," chimed in

Edward. "I hardly ever see my sister, cuz she's always off some place with you."

"Is that right, Elihu?" David eyed him narrowly.

"Yeah, sort of…I guess."

"What do you mean, 'sort of' and you 'guess?'"

Elihu shifted his weight. "I've been meaning to talk to you about her."

David blinked his eyes innocently, "Who?"

"Lizzie."

"What about Lizzie?"

"I'd like your permission to court her…sir."

David assumed an air of puzzlement.

"You want to court my daughter?"

"Yes, sir."

"How old are you, son?"

"Twenty-eight…sir."

"You do know she's only seventeen?"

"Yes, sir. But she's remarkably mature for her age."

Edward harrumphed. "You don't live with her."

"But that's exactly what I want to do…sir"

"You want to live with her?"

"Yes, sir."

"But you don't want to marry her."

"No…I mean yes. I do want to marry her."

"So you want to live with her and you want to marry her?"

"Yes, sir…to both."

"What happened to courting her?"

"Well, I want that too. I was going to start with that…you know…the courtship first, then marriage."

David looked fierce. "It seems like you want an awful lot, son."

Elihu looked stricken, then said earnestly, "Yes, I do. Your daughter means more to me than anything else in this world."

"Seeing as how you are just starting out to make a living in this world, I would say you don't have much else," David said pointedly.

"That's only true for the moment…Sir…I'm a real good carpenter and I'll do just fine and I intend to take real good care of Lizzie."

David Hardy's face relaxed and a smile appeared. "Good for you, son. I just wanted to hear you say something along those lines. And it was fun pulling your leg a wee bit too. Lizzie already spoke to me and I've had my eye on you."

He stood up and extended his hand. "You have my permission to court my daughter…and good luck."

From the sidelines, Jonathan and Edward got to their feet and shook Elihu's hand.

"You made a good move, Elihu, and you did it right proper," said Jonathan.

Edward grinned, "Before you go too far, you ought to hear some of my stories about my little sister."

* * *

In 1888, Jack the Ripper butchered two more women. During that same winter, it took several more trips across the ice to finish transporting the remaining lumber. On the last trip, Elihu met Edward Hardy at the head of the lake, and they traveled down the West Shore Road together. Just before Wellington Beach the road hugs the lake's edge and the Ledges border the right side of the road. The Ledges are a cliff formation, a couple hundred feet high, and prone to rockslides. When a slide occurred, the road was blocked off for several days until the rubble was cleared--sometimes it took several weeks.

On this occasion, as Elihu and Edward's team rounded the corner to enter the Ledges section, they startled a deer, a fine looking buck that had been browsing along the lakeside. It reared its head and stared at them for several long seconds, a frozen tableau. Then one of the horses stamped its foot and pawed the ground. The tableau shattered and the buck whirled and stotted toward the rockslide.

Edward, an avid hunter, cursed that he hadn't brought his rifle along.

The buck, having come to the slide, raced up and down its length looking for a low point to leap over. Finding none, it turned back towards them. Seeing they were still there, it doubled back to the slide.

"Elihu," exclaimed Edward, "I think we just found supper. Grab a rock or something and let's get him."

Elihu looked around and replied, "The only loose rocks are in the slide. Everything else is frozen. Might as well let him go."

"Let him go? Not a chance." Edward ran towards the buck.

Elihu shrugged his shoulders and followed him.

The buck, spotting the pursuers, ran along the slide and to the right as far as it could go until its steep angle prevented further progress. The deer reversed direction and ran down the length of the slide to where it ended in the lake. It hesitated for a moment then jumped onto the ice. Its sharp cloven hooves scrambled for purchase on the glass-like surface, slid, slipped, and the buck flopped on its belly with a whump, legs all akimbo.

"We got him now," shouted Edward. "Hurry before he gets up."

Both men raced to the frantically scrabbling buck, which was desperately attempting to regain its footing. They approached warily, careful of the slashing hooves. They circled the deer, Elihu on one side, Edward on the other.

"Well, now what?" demanded Elihu. "I didn't get a rock and you don't have any either. Sooner or later, it's going to get on its feet."

"So what? It'll just slip and fall again. It's in its nature to run and jump. With this ice, he'll just keep slippy-sliding and falling."

"We can't spend all day watching him do that. Let's just leave him."

"Not on your life are we just going to leave him. You grab his antlers and hold its head and I'll cut its throat with my pocket knife." Edward reached into his pants pocket and unfolded his knife. Its sharpened three-inch blade glittered.

"Good grief. With that little thing? Are you serious?" Elihu gaped at Edward in dismayed amazement.

"I couldn't be more so. It's only got to get in a couple inches to slice those arteries." Edward shook his head in disgust. You're not much of a hunter, are you? Now grab his head."

Edward edged toward the deer in a wrestler's crouch and motioned Elihu to move in. He did so reluctantly.

The buck followed Edward's movements, his head turning with his eyes.

"Now. Do it now," yelled Edward.

Elihu jumped on the buck's back and grabbed its antlers with both hands and pulled back, exposing its neck.

Edward jumped in and forcefully slashed down with his knife on one side of the neck and then the other. Blood sprayed, catching the front of Edward's mackinaw. The buck jerked its powerful neck back and forth causing Elihu to lose his grip. More blood sprayed. With its head no longer encumbered by Elihu's grasp, the buck slashed savagely about him with its antlers. To save himself from being skewered, Elihu pressed his head against the buck's neck and hung on as tightly as he could.

Edward yelled, "Hold him still so I can get him again."

The buck's hooves beat a tattoo on the ice, its antlers slashed the air...and then the deer began to scream--a high-pitched, piercing ululation of pure agony that rent the air and then hung there, like a trail of campfire smoke.

Edward dove onto the buck's front legs, pinning them under his weight. Then he stabbed the deer's neck, again...and again.

"Die, damn you...just die."

The spurting blood lessened. The flailing legs slowed. The once proud head sank to the ice. There was a final convulsive spasm...and then silence.

"We did it. Doggone it. We really did it," crowed Edward, standing up, his face alight with triumph.

Elihu looked at the blood staining the pristine ice and Edward's jacket, the lustrous brown eyes already dimming and glazing over, the body lifeless and limp, and said quietly, "I guess that's why I prefer fishing."

* * *

In April, 1889, the Kodak Box Camera went on sale for the first time.

Just a few weeks later, construction began on David Hardy's camp on Newfound Lake. If he or anyone in his family owned a Kodak Box Camera, they certainly would have taken several pictures to mark this momentous event, but they didn't own one yet.

Actually, Elihu, as acting supervisor, began with the barn first. It would serve as living quarters for him while working on site and a shelter for building materials and tools that had to be kept dry.

Barn raising in New England had progressed to an art and science and it didn't take but two days to put it up. The interior would be finished off later. Of course, the Hardy and Fox families showed up to help, and it was more like a festive family reunion than a work camp. Lizzie's presence didn't help Elihu's concentration and their mutual glances and smiles were noticed and commented upon by everyone.

While having lunch together on the tip of the thin peninsula, about a thousand yards from the work site--just far enough for privacy-- Lizzie asked him what he thought of the project.

"I think it's going to be a beautiful camp...in a rustic sort of way."

"Does its primitive nature concern you?"

"Not at all. I rather like it. It's simple...pure...not spoiled by too much civilization," Elihu replied.

"Good because that's exactly how I feel."

"Actually, if it were mine, I'd have it built here, right on the point where you have water on three sides and more of a view."

As far as barns go, this one was small, although it had two stories. Elihu rather enjoyed living there. Swimming in the lake after a hard day's work was heavenly.

A couple weeks later, the families returned for another weekend to help put up the framework for the camp. With the skeleton in place, Elihu could do the rest himself, beginning with the roof. It was commodious: four bedrooms upstairs, a dining room, kitchen, and living room on the first floor, and a porch on two sides--one side facing the main lake, the sunsets in the west, and benefiting from the prevailing northwesterly breezes. The side porch offered a truncated view of Mount Cardigan.

As Elihu nailed boards on walls, laid shingle on roof, snugged in windows, swam in the cove, watched sunsets, and fished from shore, he realized he was covetous--he wanted a place just like this for himself and Lizzie--right on the point.

* * *

In 1890, John Owen was the first person to run the one-hundred-yard dash under ten seconds in nine and 4/5 seconds.

Elihu Q. Sanborn was running pretty fast too. He settled into a home in Hopkington, New Hampshire, finished building the Fox/Hardy fishing camp, built up his carpentry business as quickly as possible, saved every penny he could for a camp of his own, and courted Lizzie in what time remained.

She never complained.

The following year was essentially a repeat of the previous one, except for one very important difference--on November 26th, 1891, Elihu and Lizzie got married. For a wedding present, David Hardy and Ezra collaborated and gave the young couple money toward a camp of their own.

* * *

In 1892, the US Patent Office declared J.W. Swan the inventor of the electric light carbon for the incandescent lamp rather than Thomas Edison. That wouldn't have mattered to Ezra because his own light went out earlier that year due to heart disease. Six months after Elihu's marriage, Ezra died and Simeon officially inherited the farm.

*   *   *

Two years later, Elihu and Lizzie had a baby boy. They named him Donald Edward Sanborn (who would be my Grandpa). He was their only child. He grew up shy, reticent, introspective, an observer of life around him rather than an active participant.

As far back as my grandfather could remember, most weekends were spent at Camp--with a capital "C." Camp was a proper noun to him, a special place, on a par with FDR's "beloved" Campobello, only a tad more rustic. He eagerly looked forward to going to Camp and was always sad to leave it. Elihu went to Camp to socialize with the Hardies and Foxes next door, to go fishing, and for the beauty of the Camp. My grandfather went for the beauty.

Elihu's reputation as a carpenter grew. Consequently, so did his business. Elihu must have taken Russell Cornwell's "Acres of diamonds" speech to heart because he began investing some of his money in the stock market and talking about multiple streams of income. As demand for his skills increased, his time spent at Camp decreased--much to my grandfather's disgruntlement.

Exacerbating this disgruntlement was a growing estrangement between Elihu and his son. Making money requires attention, and attention given to one thing means attention not given to another. Both Grandpa and Lizzie were shortchanged in this transaction, but Lizzie was more understanding.

So it was no surprise when the occasion arrived, when Elihu elected to work instead of going to Camp, that Grandpa asked his father and mother if he could go by himself. They decided that at age fourteen he was old enough to take the train.

* * *

On October1st, 1908, Henry Ford introduced the Model T car (cost $825). On the same day, the first Dutch electric railway went into use (Rotterdam - Hague). It was a watershed year for transportation. About the same time in New Hampshire, my grandfather sought transportation to his favorite watershed area--Newfound Lake.

Decades later, Grandpa told me this story of his first train ride to Camp.

"The train left Concord just before daybreak. I was still a youngster and growing a lot and valued my sleep more than I needed to. So I no sooner sat down on the seat but what I fell sound asleep. After a bit, the Conductor comes around to punch tickets and I'm dead to the world. He sees me and decides to have a little fun.

"He'd lost his hand to machinery while working in the Manchester woolen mills and had a steel hook fitted to his wrist stump. It was a wicked-looking thing and he took some pride in its appearance. Since then I've seen him polish it more than once.

"Well, he came up the aisle kinda quiet like and then, when he was right next to me, he banged his hook on the wooden seat by my ear and yelled, 'TICKETS!'

"Now I tell you that startled the bejeesus out of me. I about flew off that seat and almost wet myself. My eyes must have been the size of dinner plates--and right in front of them was this evil, shiny, steel hook. And this fool Conductor is laughing his butt off with this great loud, horse laugh you could hear three train cars away."

I piped up and asked Grandpa how a one-handed conductor could hold a ticket and punch it with the other hand. Wasn't it a two-handed operation?

He gave a little sigh at the interruption. "It wasn't that difficult, Lad. He'd have the passenger hold it and he'd punch it with his good hand."

"Oh," I said.

"Well, as I was saying," he continued, "about a month later I got to go by myself to Camp by train again. And this time I was ready for him."

I sat up. This was getting interesting.

"What did you do, Grandpa? Did you punch him?"

My grandfather rolled his eyes and shook his head. "No, Lad. I did him one better."

"Huh? What do you mean?" I asked.

"I pretended to fall asleep and kept my ears open. Sure enough, after a bit I heard a little scuff in the aisle behind me and I figured it was him. Then he did his banging thing with his hook and his yelling thing about the tickets and I opened one eye real slow. Then I did this full body stretch like a cat does when it gets up. Then I gave a real big yawn, as though the whole thing was a terrible bore....You should have seen his face."

Grandpa chuckled at the recollection.

"He was downright bewildered. I couldn't help myself. I busted out laughing. Then he began laughing too. We got into one of those things where the slightest thing--a look, a sound, anything--will set you off into hysterics again. After that we started to talk, and after that we became sort of friends."

"Where was the train station, Grandpa?" I asked. I had never seen one in Bristol.

Again, the barely concealed look of frustration at yet another interruption. Grandpa was chary with verbiage, but when he felt the motivation to talk, he didn't appreciate disruption. "It's long gone, Lad. The big flood of thirty-six washed out a good deal of track between Bristol and Franklin. The train company didn't want to spend the money to repair the beds and rails, so Franklin got to be the end of the line. Besides, the logging business had run its course. The whole area was bare of trees and was turned to farm land--sheep and vegetables mostly. Yup, those train days were over and done with, replaced by automobiles. Everybody had one by then."

"Do you have any car stories, Grandpa?" I asked.

"Later, Lad, I've talked enough for one day."

*　*　*

Like his father, Grandpa liked working with his hands. Following graduation from high school, he sought training as a mechanic. By age twenty-three, he was hired as such by a John Porter in Cambridge, Massachusetts. He thought the city would be exciting, perhaps even exotic--at the very least an adventure. Instead, he found life in the city a challenge-- its hustle and bustle, noise, and anonymity alien to his nature. He missed the small town ambiance of his youth and pined for the tranquility of Camp.

A wry smile tugged at the corners of his lips at the word "pine." Not so many summers ago, his mother had used that word and he asked her what it meant in the context she was using it (missing her older sister, Nettie, who had married and moved away). She told him it meant to miss someone so much that your heart ached. A few weeks later she gave him a small box wrapped up in gift paper. As she gave it to him, she said it was so he would know how much she would miss him whenever he left home. Opening the box released the resinous aroma of pine trees. Inside the box was a tiny pillow she had made and stuffed with white pine needles. The cross stitching on the pillow said, 'I pine for you and balsam too.' "Yes," he murmured, "That's exactly the right word."

His dilemma was resolved for him by President Wilson's decision to enter World War I. In 1917, Grandpa was twenty-three years old, his draft registration just filled out, and our entry into the Great War just declared. He enlisted, at least he'd have a choice of what branch of the armed services he'd be in. He selected the fledgling air force, which was caught in the middle of internecine strife--various military branches and sub groups laid claim to it. Uncle Sam transported Grandpa to San Antonio, Texas, and Lackland Air Force Base.

Grandpa stared at the flat landscape, sweated in the baking summer sun, and tried to decipher the southern drawl. He decided it was better than living in the city, but not by much. He missed the green hills of New Hampshire, especially the Camp.

His MOS (Military Occupational Specialty) was mechanic and he considered himself lucky-- he'd heard of guys drafted into the army who had been mechanics at home but were made cooks in the service and cooks who'd been made military police and police who were made clerks. He thought it asinine how often talent was ignored and skills wasted. It was like putting a square block into a round hole simply because the hole was there. Fortunately, Grandpa worked at his chosen vocation--as mechanic on the Jenny bi-plane.

The JN-4 (or Jenny) was a two-seater trainer. Each pilot sat in an open-air cockpit with nothing more than a windscreen in front for protection. Its V-8 engine developed ninety horsepower and could climb to a ceiling of four miles. During the war, nine of ten American airmen trained on them at Lackland. Grandpa worked long hours on the Jennies, keeping them aloft and their engines running smoothly and was proud of what he did.

The ace fighter pilots got all the publicity and glamour. They were the noble, shining knights of the air who, with their goggles, leather helmets, and trailing white silk scarves would clear the skyways of the dark, evil, Axis scourge. They were the new heroes…but Grandpa knew that without him and others like him, these heroes would never get off the ground.

As far as wars go, World War I was one of America's shorter ones and Grandpa returned to his New Hampshire granite hills in due course. It was time to get his life back on track.

* * *

In 1920, Babe Ruth set a home run season record with a score of fifty-four.

During that same year, another Ruth scored--

with Grandpa.

Grandpa played the violin in high school. His mother, Lizzie, required he take up a musical instrument. He could choose which one. She was determined that he be exposed to some of the finer things in life and develop some appreciation for beauty in its myriad forms. While she loved the Camp too, she wanted him to know there was life and beauty beyond the lake. While he played reasonably well, he'd never be a concert violinist.

Musical get-togethers were a common occurrence and so, fresh home from the service and trying to get reestablished, Grandpa took his violin under his arm and went to one in Concord he'd seen advertised in the paper. It was held in the basement of a Congregational church. The sounds of laughter and someone running the scales on a piano came to his ears as he descended the stairs. Entering the room, he saw a dozen people of various ages and a number of musical instruments. They seemed a cheerful, animated group. He took a chair next to the wall and began to carefully watch the crowd.

Grandpa barely made himself comfortable when a fellow started playing jazz on a saxophone. He hadn't heard much of this new music called jazz. He'd read it was gaining popularity in the cities and down south. Lizzie, however, loved classical music. Consequently, that influenced Grandpa's direction in music appreciation. She smiled proudly when he played *Clare de Lune* and the very few times he experimented with old time barn dancing fiddling, she rolled her eyes and left the room in disgust.

The saxophonist ended his piece and someone struck chords on a piano. A quartet of four women about his age at the head of the room sang, *I Hate to Get Up in the Morning*. For a moment, Grandpa was transported back to early mornings in barracks at Lackland Air Force Base. Whistles, cheers, and demands for an encore were met with a rendition of *I'm Always Chasing Rainbows*. The rich diapason of a soprano's voice rising to the rafters snatched his attention.

She was of average build with dark brown hair, more handsome than pretty. But it was her eyes he couldn't look away from. They gleamed like obsidian, shiny- black and snappy. He didn't know why that word seemed to describe them, but it was the closest he could come--snappy. He sensed her eyes could be snappy as a whip in anger or snappy with lively animation, or with laughter. He couldn't take his eyes off her.

The quartet ended and three women left. The one he had been watching stayed. The room remained quiet, expectant. She sang a solo, Mozart's *Cherubin's Aria* from *Figaro*. Grandpa never heard anything like it. Her resonant soprano flitted through the air like a hummingbird, glided like a hawk, and then, like a Valkyrie, powerfully swooped and soared toward the heavens. When she ended, the room was hushed for a few moments and then erupted in applause and whistles.

She gave a cute little curtsy and walked

through the crowd-- straight up to him, smiled, and said, "You were staring at me."

Grandpa gulped, "Yes. I wasn't trying to make you feel uncomfortable. If I did, I apologize."

"Then why were you staring?"

Grandpa decided her eyes were signaling mischief, not anger. He said, "Your voice is amazing...I only wish I could make my violin sing as beautifully," he added gallantly.

Her smile grew broader. "Well, let's find out. Play something for me."

"What? Here? Now?"

"That's why we're all here, unless you really did come to stare at us girls."

He blushed, shrugged, and bent over to remove his violin from its case. He placed it under his chin about to play when she put her hand on his arm, stopping him.

"Not here. Up there." She nodded toward the front of the room. "That's where everyone performs."

Grandpa sighed and headed in the direction indicated. She followed him. He wondered if she did so to prevent him from escaping.

"My name's Ruth. What's yours?"

"Don. My name is Don."

"Is that short for Donald?"

"Yes."

"What's your last name?"

"Sanborn."

He tried to walk faster to end the interrogation,

but the crowd had grown larger and his progress was slow.

"Where do you live?" Ruth asked.

"I live in Hopkington."

"What do you do for work?"

"I'm a mechanic. I work on engines and machines. And what do you do?" he asked, desperately hoping to shift the focus away from himself. He needn't have bothered, they had arrived at the front of the room--not soon enough for Grandpa.

"Hey, everybody. This is Don Sanborn and he's going to play the violin for us." Ruth smiled at him and said in a lower voice, "Now it's our turn to stare at you."

Grandpa usually played from sheet music. However, since Lizzie loved *Clare de Lune* so much, he'd taken the trouble to memorize it. It was the only piece he had ever memorized. And now that effort served him well as he gave a credible performance in front of Ruth and her friends.

Ruth approached him, smiling broadly. "Do you know Für Elise?"

"I've played it a couple times, but I was reading it." Grandpa looked at her suspiciously. "Why?

"Because I want you to practice it during the week and next Saturday we're going to do it as a duet together. And yes, we'll use sheet music."

Grandpa thought her pushy, but charmingly so. He responded, "I didn't know there were words to it"

"Oh, I don't think there are any words. It's just a composition."

Grandpa looked puzzled.

"I should have said before, I'm going to play the piano and you're going to accompany me on the violin."

"You play the piano too?" Grandpa asked wonderingly.

"Obviously, or we wouldn't be having this conversation," Ruth replied pertly.

Grandpa felt lightheaded and a little breathless, as though he had just run up a long flight of stairs…and he suspected he was in way over his head, but so far he didn't mind. His mother, Lizzie, had been a strong woman too, although perhaps more subtle than Ruth. It was a relationship paradigm he was used to.

* * *

In 1920, Mexican rebel, Pancho Villa, finally surrendered.

A few weeks later, Grandpa also surrendered. He was no match for Ruth Wirrell.

They often played music together--she told him when and where. She told him they were a couple-- and he agreed. It was a short courtship. She had done her assessment and found him suitable. Ruth told him they should get married--and so they did, on August 11, 1920. They honeymooned at the Camp, just as his father and mother had done. As a wedding present, Elihu and Lizzie gave them the Camp (interestingly, only Grandpa's name appeared on the transfer deed).

Lizzie spoke for herself and Elihu, "We know you love the Camp as much as we do, but because of Dad's business we can't go as often as we used to. We know you'll always take care of it."

Grandpa swore he would.

* * *

* * *

In November, the Netherlands and Germany
signed a trade agreement.

A month later, Russia and Turkey signed a non-
aggression pact.

A spirit of cooperation and negotiation was in
the air.

Ruth (who would be my grandma) liked the
Camp well enough. Certainly having waterfront
property was a status symbol. However, showing it
off to her friends presented a problem--it was so
primitive. Quaint and rustic were one thing,
outhouses and water pumps were quite another.
That had to change.

Grandpa didn't quite see the need for it, but he
did understand the need for harmony in a
relationship. He began making a list of needed
building materials.

In 1922, Grandma and Grandpa had a baby
boy, Donald E. Sanborn, Jr. (known as "Junior").
Four years later, they had another son, Robert
Sanborn (known to me as "Uncle Bob"). Both boys
went to the Camp on weekends and summer
vacations, continuing the tradition set by their
grandfather and underscored by their father.

* * *

In 1929 the Great Depression devastated the
United States and for millions, their lives changed
drastically. Grandpa and Grandma did not escape

unscathed. In 1932, Grandma's widowed mother (known as Hattie to her friends and as Mamie to family members) came to live with them. Mamie's husband, Martin, had died fourteen years ago and she went to live with her family, the Potters of East Concord. She had worn out her welcome early on, but being family, they tried to tolerate her crotchetiness. They tried for several years. But like the glacier grinding over granite bedrock, Mamie had scored and scoured them until they could take no more. She had to go--and here she came.

From the very beginning, when Grandpa first began courting Grandma, he and Mamie were like flint and steel, striking sparks whenever they were in proximity. She, like her daughter, eschewed subtlety and she made it plain that she believed Ruth could do better. And now she had come to live with them. Grandpa ground his teeth in frustration while Mamie hobbled around with her bad hip and banging her cane on the floor much louder than what was necessary--usually when Grandpa was trying to sleep.

And then Grandma's sister, Dorothy--the black sheep of the family (because she was "Divorced")-- came to live with them. Finances became tight and smiles even tighter. Grandma, who abjured the thought of penury, suggested that the Camp be sold. It was a luxury and they needed the money.

Grandpa drew a line in the sand beyond which there was no negotiation, no compromise. "The way I see it, the Camp isn't mine to sell. I'm supposed to take care of it and look after it. It belongs to the family and I'm just the custodian and manager. I'd sooner give it to Junior or Bob before I'd sell it."

Grandma's snappy black eyes narrowed, and her mouth flattened into a thin line. Her chin quivered and her face reddened. "I understand your devotion to the Camp, but you better think about your devotion to me and your family. You may be coming down to a choice between us or the Camp. We have too many mouths to feed and there's rent to pay."

Grandpa, who just that morning had exchanged caustic remarks with Mamie, said, "Then I suggest you consider reducing the number of mouths around here and look for a cheaper apartment. That's all I have to say about it." He turned and stalked away, back ramrod straight.

Grandma usually had the last word, but he was gone and the empty air was unsatisfying--in so many ways.

They did find a less expensive apartment. Dorothy found a boyfriend and moved out, saying it was time to move on. She really meant she wanted more privacy. Grandpa suppressed his disappointment that it was Dorothy who left and not Mamie. The strained atmosphere relaxed somewhat and life returned to the status quo.

* * *

Lena, who would be my mother, met Junior in

church. She remembered him from high school, where in English class, he sat a few seats catty corner behind her. He carried the reputation of an oddball. Junior certainly dressed eccentrically. He wore an old, beat up, gray fedora, and seldom removed it, even when sitting at his desk. On his feet were high-top hunting boots half-laced, and with trousers tucked in. Even stranger was the shabby, overcoat he wore--all the time. Junior seldom spoke. He usually sat in his seat with his head down. It remained unclear if he slept or simply hid himself. How the school administration allowed this bizarre behavior puzzled everyone. Lena seldom had thoughts about him, except that he was the "weird kid." When she graduated, she barely registered the fact that he hadn't.

But when she received an invitation to audition for a part in a church play entitled *The Valiant* and showed up at the North Congregational Church for tryouts, she discovered, to her astonishment, that he was the director. He struck up a conversation with her and she found him interesting rather than weird. And he kept talking. He was smooth; she was trusting. She found his attention to her hard to ignore. The more he talked and the more attention he paid, the less eccentric he seemed. Soon they were dating.

Lena heard through the grapevine that Junior had dated a girl named Rowena, so she asked him about it. He admitted going out with her a few times, but his mother didn't approve of the relationship. Lena inferred from that conversation that the Junior-Rowena duo was over. She should not have assumed.

Lena got a job with Child and Family Services. She asked him about his job. He claimed being in between jobs at the moment. That moment stretched out for months until his father and mother gave him an ultimatum: get a job or get out on your own. He reluctantly began work as a construction worker on the new Franklin Dam. He didn't like it. His father got him a job in the Bindery Department at the Rumford Press, where he worked the night shift. He didn't like that either.

The government announced its Liberty ship program to build freighters in support of the war effort. It became clear that America was becoming more involved in the European conflict. Admonitions to remind young men to register for the Draft lent an ominous note to the ongoing debate as to whether we should become more directly engaged. Certain categories of men were exempt from the Draft, but Junior didn't fit in any of them.

Junior stepped up his courting. He said he loved her mane of blond hair. Lena smiled and believed him. He said he loved her blue-gray eyes and she purred and believed that too. He said he loved her and wanted to marry her--and she melted and believed that as well. On Thanksgiving Day, November 27th 1941, they married in the church where they met.

Junior insisted they honeymoon at the Camp. He said it was a family tradition (if two such prior occasions constitute a tradition. If not then perhaps this one would make it so). She agreed, and so immediately following the holiday meal, they left in his father's car for Bristol. The light snow on the ground posed no difficulty, but the chilly night presented a challenge. They arranged two cots side by side in the dining room and fired up the Glenwood. Supper was leftover turkey and fixings heated on the top of the wood stove. Canned hash comprised another meal. They spent Thursday night through Sunday at Camp. Junior liked to walk during the day, and walk they did--for hours. At night they cuddled on the cots and got to know each other better. While their honeymoon was far from elegant, it was memorable.

Shortly after they were married, Lena met Rowena--perhaps not entirely by accident--and discovered that the new husband had visited Rowena several times over the past few months, the last occasion being the night before the wedding, when he came to say goodbye. It took a few hours.

* * *

On November 28, 1942, 492 people died in a fire that destroyed the Coconut Grove nightclub in Boston, Massachusetts.

While the Boston Fire Department tried to extinguish the blaze and save lives, about eighty miles north my mother was undergoing a trial by fire of her own--giving birth to me. She found the eight hours of labor excruciating and said if the doctor hadn't given her drugs at the end, she would have called the whole thing off.

Within days of my birth, Junior announced he didn't believe in war, killing was an anathema to him, and he shunned the bearing of arms. He was going to file as a conscientious objector. Grandpa said while he knew some people truly believed in those principles, he seriously doubted if Junior was among them. He suspected Junior was just trying to get out of something he didn't want to do--again. Grandma expressed concern about what the neighbors would think. Unless one was a minister or priest, conscientious objectors didn't rate high on the social approval scale.

Junior's commitment to his new philosophy didn't last very long. Perhaps due to a change of heart or maybe social pressure, he changed his mind and five months after I was born, he boarded a train for New York City to enlist in the Merchant Marines. He left within weeks for the Maritime Training Academy.

Junior sometimes came home on leave, sometimes not. When he did, his attentiveness was less than it used to be, his professions of love and commitment less frequent and poetic. On one occasion, in which he did come home, my mother was cleaning out his pockets, prefatory to washing his clothes, when she found a slip of paper with a woman's name, address, and telephone number. She lived in England, one of Junior's ports of call. A confrontation occurred. Junior told my mother that if she persisted in going through his things, she might not like what she found.

"In war time men had certain needs, the fulfillment of which had nothing to do with marriage," he said.

My mother was not pleased.

On August 31, 1945, my sister, Lea, was born. Junior went back to sea.

Perhaps it was retributive justice that my mother found comfort, companionship and understanding with Junior's best friend. It didn't take long for this relationship to be discovered and a separation ensued, followed by a divorce in 1946. My mother took my sister and went with her new love. Junior remained in the Merchant Marines, and I was given to the care of my grandparents.

* * *

In fact, experience is just another word for baggage. And memory carries the bags.
     —Nelson Demille, The Gate House

Grandpa and Grandma saw no reason to alter their established pattern of going to Camp on weekends and vacation and so, from as far back as I can remember, that became a major part of my life. I splashed in those magical lake waters, reveled in the resinous smell of the giant pine trees, picked blueberries, developed a love of boats-- and I listened to the stories, gossip, comments, and retorts as the adults reminisced, complained, and bragged. Through six generations these stories, as told and retold by various family members, became part and parcel of the Camp legends, which to my young mind, frequently attained mythic proportions.

I'm sure there were many more stories to tell, but no one thought to write them down at the time, and over time memories fade and falter, and some were relegated to the shame-shrouded land of "we don't ever talk about that outside the family…" It seems to be a universal generality that while the old want to reminisce, the young are too busy living to bother.

For good or ill, memories freeze a person in time and place, anchor a person in heritage and relationships, and provide a template for understanding--to be utilized or not. What I would give now to have asked questions then, to come across old letters, diaries, or journals--or in my wildest fantasies to reanimate the dead for a fireside chat. But they are all gone now: Ezra, Elihu and Lizzie, Grandpa and Grandma, Uncle Bob, Roy, Mamie and Mr. Irving--the principle players in the first half of my life. It is my hope that in these pages, I have brought them all to life once more to strut and fret their hour upon the stage.

THE OUTHOUSE

It has been said the health of a civilization is determined in part by the efficacy of its sanitation efforts. These efforts have generally focused on the transporting of potable water and the removal of human waste. The might of the Roman Empire was aided and abetted in no small measure by its innovative sanitation system of gutters, sluiceways, conduits, aqueducts, sewers, cisterns, settling basins, large cemented reservoirs, and baths. Public latrines in Rome were unisex, consisting of long bench-like seats with keyhole-shaped openings to sit over. A trench with running water carried away the waste. Unlike today, where public toilets usually offer privacy and an opportunity to catch up on reading, the Roman public latrine had no privacy and was often seen as a place to socialize.

During the Middle Ages in London, streets were constructed so that they either had a central gutter running down the middle or they had lateral gutters for run-off water and slops. In 1596, John Harrington invented the flush toilet and in 1778 Joseph Bramah of Yorkshire patented the first practical water closet in England. In the 1880's Thomas Crapper gained repute as one of the leading purveyors of flush toilets and water closets.

Thomas Crapper's water closet consisted of a container of water situated several feet above the toilet. Pulling on a chain would release the water down a pipe into the toilet bowl, flushing the effluent away through sewage pipes to another destination. The usual destination for many years was a nearby river.

During my early years living with my grandparents, the toilet in their house was of the Thomas crapper style. Its overhead water reservoir was set under the bathroom ceiling and directly over the toilet. The reservoir itself was enclosed in a wooden box, matching in style and color the bathroom's wainscoting. A thin chain with a wooden handle resembling a pine cone hung from the reservoir. Pulling on this chain would release gallons of water in a roaring rush down the pipe to swirl into the toilet bowl beneath, carrying all away in a surging, boiling commotion. As a child, I had fears of being swept away in the maelstrom, which led to subsequent accusations of failure to flush.

*　*　*

My first few years at Camp found it in much the same condition as it was when my great-grandfather gave it to my grandparents as a wedding gift: a large rambling fishing shack with no modern conveniences. Arguably, the most inconvenient missing convenience was the lack of an indoor toilet.

What served the purpose stood seventy-five feet away, a gray, weather-beaten, barn board-covered outhouse, discreetly screened by white pine, swamp maple, and varieties of underbrush. It featured a utilitarian one-holer design. The structure rested upon a single layer foundation of native rock, raising it a foot above ground level. The top four inches between its walls and the wooden roof were screened for ventilation. Sitting on the bench beside the open hole (a thin, square board covered the hole when not in use) was a metal bucket containing wood ash from the Camp's Glenwood. The ash, when sprinkled down the hole after doing one's business, served to reduce the odor and kept the flies away. This seemed to work well.

I still remember my grandfather's cautionary advice to bang on the bench with my hand before sitting down, "You don't want to get bit by a spider, Lad. It hurts and they're nasty." I never did get bit, but I often wondered if that might be why Grandma was afraid of spiders.

On the other side of the bench was a roll and a spare of toilet paper. Grandma was not one for the stereotypical Sears and Roebuck catalogue pages, except to order from, and she was not one to be caught short. Grandpa, on the other hand, who never ordered from the catalogue, would have found the outhouse an appropriate use for it. However, in matters such as these, he judiciously deferred to Grandma.

The unspoken protocol was that from wake-up until bedtime, one used the outhouse during the day, and using the outhouse during the day was no great inconvenience, unless it was raining. For those middle of the night emergencies, however, a different protocol was utilized: the "thunder jug."

The thunder jug was an enameled metal chamber pot with a lid which upon arising was carried to the outhouse and emptied. I remember as a child giggling at the improbable image of my grandmother's portly bulk teetering on the thunder jug in the middle of the night. I can't imagine how she did it, but I know she did because on many a morning's dash to the outhouse, I passed her returning to the Camp, empty jug in hand.

My father and Uncle Bob spent their youth at Camp on weekends and summer vacations, as did I. They used the outhouse, as did I. They were also raised with my live-in great-grandmother. Everyone called her, Mamie.

In spite of having to walk with a cane, due to an ill-healed fractured hip, Mamie was a force of nature, like my grandmother, only more formidable. For reasons unknown to me, she and my grandfather shared a mutual antipathy for each other. She, like my grandmother, was not one to repress her dislikes, and she often unabashedly vented her displeasure with my grandfather by well-placed caustic remarks. To be fair, he was once heard calling her "an old harpy" under his breath.

One of Mamie's most salient characteristics was her sense of patriotism. She was adamantine in her belief that the President, all things governmental, especially the Armed Services, and most especially, the American flag, were to be respected. Not a parade could pass by but she would poke my father and Uncle Bob in the back with her cane and tell them to stand up and put their hands over their hearts in salute. Whenever the "Star Spangled Banner" was heard, she would order my father (everyone called him Junior) and Uncle Bob to "Stand up, tall and proud. Show them you're proud to be an American." I never knew who "they" were, but whoever they were, I'm sure they were duly impressed by the alacrity with which Junior, Uncle Bob, and Mamie bounded to their feet, clasped right hands over their respective hearts, and exuded fierce American patriotism as the Flag wafted by and the stirring strains of the "Star Spangled Banner" swelled their very souls with pride.

* * *

The moment she was introduced to the phonograph by a friend, Grandma knew she had to have one. To hear the voices of the great Caruso or Lily Pons, to hear the divine majesty of Handel's Hallelujah chorus from the "Messiah," this was heaven-sent. In short order grandma was the proud owner of one. This would certainly make Camp-life more tolerable. And so it was that Sigfried's Rhine Journey came to the lake and the Halls of the Mountain King reverberated within the walls of the Camp.

Now, four seemingly disparate elements were brought into proximity: the outhouse, Mamie, the phonograph, and Junior - or rather Junior's devious mind. Perhaps he had been to one too many parades with Mamie, or perhaps he was merely looking for a little excitement, but in any event, Junior put two and two together and came up with his inimitable seven. He drew his brother aside and excitedly divulged his Machiavellian plot. Uncle Bob, as usual and against his better judgment, became ensnared by Junior's enthusiasm, his fast-talking glibness, and the sheer audacity of the plan.

The week before they were scheduled to leave for Camp for the Memorial Day weekend, Junior and Uncle Bob pooled their allowance monies, made the necessary purchases, and secreted their acquisitions in their suitcase, which was already packed. They revised their plans several times, or rather Junior did and Uncle Bob concurred. Frequently they were observed in a huddle, giggling conspiratorially. Grandpa figured the boys were up to something. Grandma thought it was sweet the boys were getting along so well. Mamie was preoccupied with her chronic gastrointestinal ailment and was oblivious to the boys - and it was this very ailment that played a major role in Junior's latest nefarious scheme.

The boys' plan was scheduled for implementation on Sunday because on that day everyone would be following their normal Camp relaxation routine. The boys knew Saturday was going to be a long day filled with frustrated anticipation - and so it was. It began with Mamie spending longer than usual in the bathroom, delaying their start. Traffic was heavy so the trip to Camp seemed endless. Although Mamie's remarks that some drivers were slower than cold molasses and if we had left earlier (conveniently ignoring the fact that she was the cause of the delay), we'd be there by now had the potential for enlivening the trip, but Grandpa wisely ignored the bait.

It seemed as though everyone in town and around the lake had decided to shop at the First National store at the same time. Finally they arrived at Camp and Grandma, ever the cruise director, told Grandpa to take their suitcase up to their bedroom and then put the phonograph in the living room. The boys were to take care of their and Mamie's suitcases and then put the groceries away. Mamie would set the table and Grandma would start to prepare lunch.

The afternoon dragged on for the boys. Grandma listened to a recording of "Carmen" on the phonograph. Grandpa listened to the ballgame on the crystal radio on the porch. The Red Sox were playing at Fenway Park. Mamie snoozed noisily in her rocking chair, her cane across her lap, as though at the ready. Junior and Uncle Bob rotated from playing horseshoes, to playing catch, to horsing around in the swimming area. Occasional bursts of laughter punctuated the whispered conversations between the two only confirmed Grandpa's earlier suspicion that they were conniving some scheme.

Supper ended and they all settled down to the

usual evening's pattern of board games. That night it was Flinch. The boys, keyed up and preoccupied with their plans for the morrow, made careless mistakes, prompting Grandma to query, "What's going on with you two? You're not paying any attention at all. Have you done something you should be telling me about?" This was greeted by nervous laughter and furtive smiles at each other.

Junior immediately assumed the air of injured innocence and declared they were just tired from a long day and playing hard outside all afternoon. Uncle Bob readily nodded his head in agreement.

"Well then," said Grandma, "You might as well go to bed."

They did so without protest, further confirming Grandpa's suspicions.

* * *

Grandpa was an early riser on the weekends. He looked forward to an hour or so of delicious solitude and sipping his first cup of coffee without interruption or distraction. He especially enjoyed it when his mother-in-law slept late. So when he spied Junior and Uncle Bob surreptitiously creeping down the stairs with two packages in hand, he was first annoyed, then curious, and then very suspicious.

"Hold it right there, you two." His voice wasn't loud, but it cut the early morning air like a whip and froze the boys in their tracks. "What's in those packages and where do you think you're going?" he demanded.

Junior, seldom at a loss for words, spluttered and stammered. Uncle Bob looked like a deer frozen in the headlights. Junior tried to talk and stammered again. Taking a deep breath he tried once more. He explained how it was Memorial Day weekend, and knowing how patriotic Mamie was, he and Bob had bought a small American flag and they were going to place it outside, someplace. They were just going out to find the best place, and since this was to be a surprise for Mamie, would he keep it a secret?

Grandpa , still mistrustful and unmollified, said, "Show me this flag." Junior removed the cap from the end of a two-foot cardboard tube and drew out an American flag, the very same that every hardware store in every town and city sold just before Memorial Day for families to put on the graves of their deceased veterans.

Now, somewhat mollified, but still a bit suspicious, Grandpa said, "Okay. Now what's in the other package you're hiding?"

Exchanging glances with his co-conspirator, Junior said, "We all know how much Mom enjoys listening to her music here at Camp and since Bob and I were in a buying mood, we decided to buy a recording for her, and it's a surprise as well, so we hope you would be willing to keep it a secret too."

This thoughtfulness was so unlike the boys, or Junior anyway, but Grandpa was no fool. "Show me this recording," he demanded. Dutifully, Junior reached into the brown paper bag Bob was holding and withdrew a recording encased in its cardboard jacket. Grandpa couldn't see the label the way Junior held it, but it definitely looked like a new recording. "I'll be damned," muttered Grandpa as the surprised look in his eyes turned to reluctant respect. "I wouldn't have guessed this in a hundred years. Go to it, boys. I'll keep your secret." The boys raced outside.

Sunday morning breakfast at Camp was traditionally a special event: lots of eggs, both scrambled and fried, lots of bacon, hash brown potatoes with chopped onion, toast and jam, dry cereal of various kinds, and when in season, slices of cantaloupe. Sometimes it was French toast or pancakes with maple syrup. Grandpa was a moderate eater, as was Junior. In fact, moderation in all things could be said to be Grandpa's credo. Grandma was a big eater - except at breakfast - as her abdominous girth suggested. Mamie was also a big eater, but she paid for the pleasure by spending a while in the bathroom afterwards. Uncle Bob was the biggest eater of all - prodigious would be more accurate - but he was still young, active, and slender. That Sunday morning he ate much less than usual, causing Grandma to ask if he was feeling all right. Uncle Bob averred that he was just eager to get outside in the sunshine. Grandma looked skeptical, but let it pass. In her mind, how one was eating was a direct gauge of one's state of health, a pathognomonic indicator of some disease or bodily dysfunction.

With breakfast finished, Grandma and Grandpa went to the kitchen to do dishes. Junior motioned to his brother to engage Mamie in conversation while he sidled into the living room, cradling Grandma's phonograph in his arms, and crept outside.

The brief sound of a hammer pounding outside signaled Uncle Bob to end his chit-chatting with Mamie and join his brother. Now it was just a matter of waiting.

They didn't have long to wait. Mamie's cane could be heard tapping on the stone path as she made her predictable post-prandial journey to the outhouse. The boys were hiding, crouched behind Grandpa's car, their eyes glued on Mamie's slow perambulation. As she opened the outhouse door there was a quick glimpse of an American flag stapled to the inside of the door. When she turned around and sat down she would be staring eye-level at the Stars and Stripes.

Junior, phonograph clutched to his chest, dashed to the front of the outhouse and carefully set it on the ground. Uncle Bob joined him just as his brother engaged the controls and stood up. Within seconds the opening strains of the "Star Spangled Banner" blared out of the phonograph: "Oh say can you see…" the slam of the porch door was heard in the distance as Grandpa and Grandma bustled out of the Camp to see what the commotion was all about.

Junior wagged his forefinger three times in front of his brother and the words, "One, two, three…" and in unison they shouted their well-rehearsed lines: "Stand up, Mamie. Standup and salute the flag. Show you're proud to be an American." They convulsed with laughter and pounded each other on the back.

Grandma exclaimed, "What in the world…"

Grandpa looked at Junior and pointed at the outhouse door, "The flag…there?" Junior nodded as he laughed.

"The bombs bursting in air…" Junior yelled, "Are you standing up, Mamie?"

Uncle Bob, in imitation of his brother, yelled, "Is your hand over your heart, Mamie?"

As Grandpa stood there, taking it all in, a look of understanding and appreciation came into his eyes, and a smile began to play along his lips. The smile grew, and then he laughed… and laughed until the tears came.

Grandma, looking bewildered, demanded, "Will someone please tell me what's going on?"

The last stanza echoed in the morning air, "And the home of the brave."

THE HONOLULU CONNECTION

My grandparent's summer cottage hosted three objects completely alien to its Yankee ambiance, their nature as foreign as some extraterrestrial artifact. However, as I had grown up with them as an integral part of the Camp's surroundings, I gave little thought to their unique nature until I was well into middle school.

The first object -- a cape of beaten tree bark about four-foot square and marked with arcane glyphs scorched into its surface -- was fastened to the living room wall like a tapestry. When a north wind blew down the lake the frequent draft that weaseled its way under the outside door caused the cape's surface to ripple and shimmy.

Displayed as an *objet trouvé* on top of the oak credenza in the dining room, lay an ovoid-shaped stone about half the size of a football, black as a crow's wing, silky smooth to the touch, and deeply honeycombed. The rock's lightness always surprised me; it appeared much heavier than its actual weight.

The third item was a foot-and-a-half long wooden ceremonial war club. The wood, heavy, hard, and a deep red mahogany color had small white, diamond-shaped inlays, whether shell, bone, or ivory, I couldn't tell. A knife's edge ran along one side of the shank. Grandma tucked the war club away inside the credenza, as though she didn't quite know what to do with it, or what to say about it.

Perhaps its display was not deemed to be politically correct, but she couldn't bring herself to dispose of it either (her attic was jam-packed with such questionable memorabilia and indecision).

Whether I learned of these objects provenance in one long winter night's tale or in dribs and drabs from various family members over time, I don't recall, but according to Camp legend the following is their accounting:

Grandma had a younger brother whom she adored. Paul, in turn, treated her more as an equal and confidante than just an older sister. Her sororal love for him had more than a modicum of possessiveness and when he came of an age to go a-courting, Grandma had difficulty sharing him. Apparently Paul managed to assuage her miffed feelings to the point where they could discuss his gal of the moment, Grandma's toleration of them being predicated on the assumption that their entanglement with her brother's time and affection was only temporary.

That understanding worked for a while until Paul met and fell deeply in love with a young woman from the Concord area. Her name, appearance, and mannerisms are not mentioned in the Camp legend, but it is noted that it wasn't long before Paul approached the young lass's father and respectfully beseeched him for her hand in marriage and was soundly rejected. Paul was told by the not-to-be father-in-law he would never amount to much, his daughter deserved better, and to put an end to his courting.

Devastated and reeling with wounded pride, Paul returned home. Grandma asked him what he was going to do. He didn't know. He hadn't considered that his suit would be denied; he had told his friends that he was going to marry her. Knowing she was now unobtainable, he couldn't bear to see her again - nor could he face his friends. He decided to leave his hometown and travel as far from the Granite State as he possibly could. He packed his suitcase, kissed Grandma and family goodbye and took Horace Greeley's advice and headed west.

For a while Paul's family received a postcard or letter every couple of weeks as he worked his way across the country, but after a few months his correspondence dwindled to once a month, and then less. Grandma and the family infrequently wrote Paul because he seldom stayed at any one place long enough to establish an address.

Grandma never forgave the young lass or the father either, for that matter. Her feelings for her brother gradually shifted from adoration to ambivalence. She could understand his leaving in his grief; she could not understand why he stayed away and continued westward. She began to feel rejected and abandoned herself. She missed him terribly and she was becoming angry with him. Her protector and confidante had deserted her.

* * *

War raged in Europe as WWI continued to slog its way through the muddy fields and shattered forests of France. That was probably one of the last wars still romanticized and Paul, ever the romantic, enlisted. Working his way across America had far less *éclat* than his willingness to transmute his grief from rejection into willingness to lay down his life for his country. He joined the Navy. His letter home elicited some pride over their son in uniform -- probably his very intent on some level -- and a good deal more anxiety. Grandma found this military image of Paul went a long way in assuaging her feelings of desertion. Also, the fact that her fiancé, my future grandfather, had just enlisted in America's fledgling Air Force gave further élan to Paul's new-found patriotism.

The new Navy base at Pearl Harbor, Hawaii, became his permanent station. He fell in love with his new home: the sun-drenched tropical islands, the verdant volcanic slopes and valleys lush with riotous colors, the white and black sandy beaches, and the ingenuous friendliness of its Polynesian inhabitants - all in all, the antithesis of his cold and dour New England heritage.

Whenever he had leave, Paul went exploring and his letter writing productivity grew apace with his explorations. He took a boat from Oahu to neighboring Maui and spent three days on the newly built Hana Highway, basically a jeep trail with the most amazing hairpin curves, precipitous drop-offs bordering the road's edge, its countless waterfalls, and the spectacular Haleakala Crater, which, he exclaimed in a letter home, was almost twice as high as New Hampshire's Mount Washington, its crater larger than the island of Manhattan, and whose alien landscape resembled what he imagined the surface of the moon to be like. While Mount Washington's summit was capped with snow much of the time, so too was Mount Haleakala's summit capped with white -- not with snow, but with the silversword plant, whose silver-white leaves from a distance appeared as snow. The silversword lives fifteen to fifty years and blooms only once, sending a stalk five to six feet upwards -- then it dies. Upon learning this, Paul felt the silversword symbolized his unrequited love for his Concord lass. His melancholy at this imperfect metaphor was deepened when he learned that wild goats were eating the plant to extinction. Fortunately, his mood was disrupted by the sight of a snaking river of petrified black lava that had debouched out of the crater and slithered down the mountainside straight into the ocean.

He took a side trail, one of many, off the Hana Road and came out on a curving black sand beach. Near the tree line the littoral was mostly composed of small, black stones worn smooth by the ceaseless pounding of waves over the millennia. The stones were obviously from the lava flow and were riddled with small holes like a petrified sponge -- nothing at all like New Hampshire's granite field stones. He selected one about half the size of a football and decided to box it up and send it home. Paul thought his family would find it a curio of interest….and he hoped every time they looked at it they would remember him. When he showed the lava rock to a shipmate, he became momentarily disconcerted to hear that the Hawaiian goddess, Pele, took umbrage at those who would pilfer her land. His shipmate appeared only half-joking when he told Paul that if his world suddenly took a turn for the worse, he could blame it on Pele's revenge…and she often took years to exact it. Paul mailed the package anyway.

Sometime later he took another trip, this time to the island of Kauai, reputed to be the wettest place on earth, a lush rain forest that saw rain every day of the year, He traversed the shoulder of a soaring volcanic mountain on a foot-wide goat path, scuttling sideways like a crab facing the mountain, his heels an inch or two from a sheer seven hundred foot drop to the crashing waves below. The path ended on the Na Pali coast, famed for its cavernous sea caves. One such smaller cave was about twenty feet wide, fifteen feet tall and extended into the mountain at least a hundred feet. The floor was flooded with a full fathom of sea water. At the far end of the cave was a tiny sandy beach. The sunlight reflected through the water and off the sandy bottom, allowing Paul to easily see his way to swim to the beach, where he lay on his back resting, watching the play of reflected sunlight on the cave's walls and ceiling.

He wrote home about the torch-lit luau he attended on the beach: the succulent pig roasted over a pit, and the native dish of poi -- the pork was wonderful, the poi tasteless -- the native dances with the women in grass skirts shimmying in a most delightful manner. The men in loin cloths and capes of beaten tree bark pranced and gyrated in what might be mock combat or a bad case of Saint Vitus dance. And did they know that ukulele in Hawaiian meant leaping flea? Paul later managed to persuade one of the male dancers to sell his cloak for a few good American dollars. He sent the cape home to his folks for a Christmas present.

Open air markets are commonplace throughout Polynesia and in Honolulu, which hosted a naval base, an army base, and an air force base, it was a given -- a ready supply of U.S. service men on weekend leave with money to spend. It was while strolling through one such market that Paul spied a ceremonial war club similar to those he had seen brandished by male dancers at the Luau. A perfect souvenir from his new home to his family in his old home.

* * *

WWI had long ended. Over the years Paul had dated sporadically but always trepidatiously - afraid to commit, afraid of rejection. His friends had given up any efforts at matchmaking and resigned themselves to the probability that he would remain a bachelor. Meanwhile, Grandpa married Grandma, sired two sons - my father and Uncle Bob - and struggled through the depression. After her husband died, Grandma's mother, known as Mamie, came to live with them. While Mamie and Grandpa disagreed over almost everything, they usually managed to maintain an uneasy truce. Then Grandma's sister, Dorothy, the perennial scapegoat and black sheep of the family also came to live with them following a divorce. The rumblings of disquiet within the household were only matched by the rumblings of imminent war in Europe.

Uncle Bob, entered his junior year of high school and wearily trudged from one academic subject to another. He let it be known that he wanted to drop out of school and join the Armed Services, perhaps the Navy, like his Uncle Paul, whom he had never met but whom Mamie and his mother talked about now and then. Grandma and Grandpa told him in no uncertain terms that he would graduate high school first and then his life was his own to direct. Uncle Bob sitzkrieged through his senior year of high school and finally graduated. Keeping to their word, my grandparents reluctantly allowed him to enlist in the Navy. His brother had already joined the Merchant Marines.

* * *

Eventually Paul met, dated, and fell in love with a slender Japanese girl living nearby. It probably helped that her father had passed away two years previously. She and another young Japanese woman shared an apartment. There was no one to deny his suit except the young woman herself. They married on December sixth, 1941 in a quiet ceremony with only one of Paul's shipmates and his bride's roommate in attendance. The next morning, and their first morning as a honeymoon couple, was heralded by the screaming roar of diving airplanes with the decal of the rising sun on their fuselages, the deafening, thunderous concussion of exploding bombs, and the ululating wail of various sirens: air raid, police, and ambulance.

Paul's world collapsed, as it did for most people in Hawaii. Martial law was declared and continued for three years. A curfew was strictly enforced. All persons of Japanese heritage were suspect and investigated. Paul's wife was interrogated at length.

On the mainland fear of the "Yellow peril" struck deep in the heart of America. Patriotism soared to an all-time high and racial discrimination and loathing soared apace. Grandpa and Grandma, who had fretted over Junior's safety on the Atlantic shipping lanes now broadened their concern to Uncle Bob in the Pacific. The newswires carried horrific stories of fanatical Kamikaze pilots intentionally driving their explosives-laden planes in suicidal plunges into American ships, Japanese atrocities, their barbaric P.O.W. camps, and their mindless and godless devotion to their heathen emperor in a place called the Forbidden City. It didn't matter that the Forbidden City was in China and they had the wrong emperor. They were all the same. Anyone with an epicanthal fold was suspect. Similar hysterical hyperbole was splashed daily across America's headlines. Internment camps were hastily constructed in the western half of the United States. Tens of thousands of U.S. citizens of Japanese descent were interned. During the entire war only ten people were convicted of spying for Japan and, ironically, these were all Caucasian.

Life in America was radically altered: shortages of food, metals, rubber, paper, petroleum products, textiles, and more became an everyday expectation. Rationing became a way of life. Waiting lines were the rule. The Draft exacted its toll in young men's bodies and their loved ones' heartache. The young were shipped off and their caskets shipped home. Rosie the Riveter manned the home front and for the first time women joined the workforce in droves and forever changed the face of womanhood in America. War bond rallies were held. Flags flew everywhere.

Soon enough Grandma received a letter from Uncle Bob. He was alright - just barely. He was aboard the aircraft carrier USS Wasp as a signalman. He wrote that at high noon (the date was blacked out) he was below decks waiting in the chow line, almost ready to be served, when he was ordered by the bridge to report topside. A formation of American fighters was returning and his signalman duties were required ASAP. Cursing, (remember, he hadn't eaten) he returned his tray and silverware and made his way up the ladders to the flight deck, where he grabbed his flags and helped guide the formation, one by one, down onto the deck.

No sooner had the last fighter landed when out of the sky, where they had been dog tailing the Americans at a barely discernible distance, a formation of Japanese fighters came swooping down. They strafed the parked planes and antiaircraft placements and then bombed the ship. One particularly devastating bomb slammed onto and penetrated the flight deck and exploded below decks in the chow hall, exactly in the area where Uncle Bob usually sat. If he hadn't been called topside, he and his fried spam and mashed potatoes would have been blown to bits, like several of his shipmates.

The letter fluttered to the table. Grandma was speechless, for a change. Grandpa slowly shook his head, took off his wire rim glasses and wiped his eyes. Both were appalled and heartsick. The slant-eyed heathen had almost killed their boy.

A few days later, in one of those ironic twists of fate that cause one to wonder if there is a higher power, and if so, then is it benignant or maleficent or just not paying attention, another letter came. This one, much delayed, came from Paul, proudly announcing his forthcoming wedding on the

morrow to his lovely, soon-to-be Japanese bride….
It could not have been more ill-timed. Grandma, in
an instant rage, declared Paul was consorting with
the enemy and she would never write or have
anything to do with him again. This was the last
time he would betray her.

Paul, unaware that Grandma had declared him
dead to her, continued to write the occasional letter,
but now it was Mamie who read them aloud. At
those times when Mamie read one of Paul's letters,
Grandma would make a show of disdainfully
withdrawing, although not entirely out of earshot.
Her outward demeanor of indifference was belied
by the intense look of concentration in her eyes as
she surreptitiously strained to hear every word.

I was in the second grade when Mamie died.
Dorothy had left the household a few years back for
another husband. Paul's annual Christmas
newsletter arrived amidst a passel of other
Christmas cards and bills. Grandma held it in her
hands. There was no one else of the family left to
read it to. She took it to her room. And so began the
rebirth of her correspondence with her brother, an
annual newsletter in which she never inquired or
made mention of Paul's wife.

Grandma was in her mid-seventies when
Grandpa passed away from too many years of
unfiltered Camels and the crescive disappointments
with his life. Now Grandma could do what she had
always wanted to do but didn't feel she could
before. Grandpa's idea of travel hadn't extended

much further than the Camp, although once, in his friskier days, he had taken Grandma to Niagara Falls. Grandma went to Venice, and complained of too many cussed bridges (her legs weren't what they used to be). She went to Oberammergau, Germany to witness the Passion Play, but it was too long and the seats too hard. And she flew to Honolulu and was reunited with her brother. Upon her return, she grudgingly admitted that Paul's wife, "seemed very nice."

MR. IRVING

I was young, about ten years old. He was old, probably as old as God, and just as smart. He lived by himself in a house that he had built with his own skilled hands. Built into the side of a hill just above the lake, it was shaded and shrouded by trees, white pine and hemlock, and barely visible by lake or the dirt road that passed by it. In curious juxtaposition to this seclusiveness was a substantial cemented seawall that girded his lakefront property, reminiscent of the bailey of a feudal castle. A pale yellow boathouse squatted over the seawall's opening like a seagull on a ridge pole - solitary, defiant and patently obvious. And this, perhaps better than anything else, symbolized a veritable sea of contradictions in this solitary gentleman, who, for reasons unknown to anyone - perhaps even himself - took a liking to me.

He was large physically, and larger than life in presence. The grey neck of Long Johns could be seen under his red and black checked shirt, which he wore summer and winter. Baggy grey trousers were supported by suspenders over a substantial girth. Tan construction boots shod his feet. On his head perched a red and black hunting hat with earflaps tied up. On the front of his hat was affixed a peanut butter jar's screw cap, upon which was printed in black letters, "Get out of UN." Whether this was a political statement directed towards the USA or the USSR was ambiguous. People seldom asked for clarification. On most matters, there was little doubt where he stood.

He was known locally as the hermit, an old coot, a lunatic, and by those kinder souls in town as an eccentric, but harmless. My grandparents called him "Mr. Irving" and their summer camp was a scant third of a mile down the dirt road.

Just how Mr. Irving became an integral part of our family Camp's legend has been lost in history, but tales told relate that when my great grandfather came to build his fishing shack on the point of land, Mr. Irving appeared out of nowhere to help him, and then just as abruptly disappeared. My grandfather remembered him featuring large in his own youthful summers at Camp, as did my father. And now my initiation was at hand.

Mr. Irving usually visited us about three times during the summer season, the first time would be about mid-June. Having finished supper, my grandparents and I usually sat on the screened-in porch playing checkers or Flinch. From the water I heard a soft shuga, shuga, shuga. Mr. Irving's long, white Cape Dory style motor boat glided into shore and we traipsed down the stone walkway to greet him at our swimming area.

Clambering over the craft's side - no easy feat for my portly grandmother - we would set out to sedately cruise the perimeter of the lake. I'd ask Mr. Irving to tell me again how he made his boat go so quietly when all the other motorboats were louder than cars without mufflers. He'd smile indulgently, disregarding my grandparent's admonitions that I had heard the story so many times before that I should by now have it memorized. Mr. Irving patiently described how he had taken an engine out of an Oldsmobile and with block and tackle had installed it in his boat. He had handcrafted a muffler the way they should be made so he wouldn't have to put up with that infernal racket that most motorboats emitted. I marveled that he could do such things.

It always astonished me that for a hermit, who supposedly avoided people, he knew more about what was going on around the lake than my grandparents. He informed us about who owned what cottage, often what they did for work and where. I remember wondering why so many cottage-owners lived so far away, and why so many were from out of state.

The trips were usually timed so that we returned just after dark, the running lights glowing red, green and white and that wonderful engine purring shuga, shuga, shuga. Sometimes in the dim of twilight we could see the flitting forms of bats swooping in the air and my grandmother would give a little gasp and put her hands over the kerchief she wore to prevent them from becoming entangled in her hair. My grandfather would put his arm around her protectively and pat her arm reassuringly while Mr. Irving once again informed us about the bat's marvelous sonar system which enabled them to unerringly fly about on the darkest nights gobbling tons of pesky mosquitoes and never colliding with anything. Grandma, cowering into my grandpa's protective shoulder, never heard a word. I knew that she was ready to be back at camp, sitting at the card table playing Flinch.

A few times, on evening excursions, we saw the Northern lights and Mr. Irving gave us lengthy explanations as to what caused these mysterious waves of yellow- green illuminations as they shifted, corrugated, and circumvoluted in the night sky. I don't remember a word he said, but I remember I knew without a doubt that if I ever had to know anything about anything, he would know the answer.

It became my habit, after awakening at camp and having breakfast with my grandparents, to say I was going to visit Mr. Irving. Grandma would tell me to be back for lunch and I would set out on the dirt road leading to his cottage.

He was always reading whenever I arrived. He'd set aside his book or newspaper and ask me if I was ready. I'd nod in the affirmative. He would heave his bulk out of his beat-up, horsehair-stuffed chair and pass me an empty onion bag that he had placed on the footstool in anticipation of my arrival. We'd descend the shaded path to where his seawall ended and the sandy beach began.

The beach, a crescent of golden sand perhaps a thousand feet long faced the prevailing breeze from the North. As we performed our morning patrol of the water's edge, there was usually a small handful of washed up dead fish, which I put in the onion bag. Mr. Irving collected the driftwood. During our peripatetic collection route, he would explain the various causes of fish death: old age, disease, fishermen throw-aways, and so on. These and a hundred other topics - most of which I paid scant attention to - were cast before me.

We returned to the lee side of his boathouse, where he had two, four-foot raised bed gardens, all enclosed in a five-foot chicken-wire fence. I had never seen or heard of raised beds. I thought gardens were supposed to grow in straight rows with the seed package attached to a stake at the end of each row. As he prepared his morning tea, Mr. Irving explained the effects of soil compaction versus aeration, moisture depth on root growth, compost versus commercial fertilizer, soil microbes, manual pollination versus bee pollination , and on he went. What impressed me the most at the time was his three-wheeled cart, upon which he sat and rolled between his raised beds, squashing a pest bug between his fingers here or pulling the infrequent weed there.

My job was to take his hatchet and chop each dead fish into two-inch pieces and plant them in the raised beds between the vegetables. Mr. Irving told me again how the early settlers had learned from the Indians the value of fish fertilizer and how later Americans, seldom learning from their profligate ways, had almost fished the American Shad to extinction to fertilize thousands of acres with tons of the so-called "trash" fish. He said the same disregard for the environment was going on as he was speaking with the sperm whale, which was tottering on the verge of annihilation because of the demand for margarine, cattle fodder, dog food, glue and leather preservatives. This led to a disquisition on the obliteration of the western plains buffalo and then to an exegesis on and a declamation of the Capitalist system. I thought about going for a swim.

While I fertilized his raised beds, he did his patient and level best to teach me about the world around me. These informal times of instruction often coincided with his morning tea, and his morning tea ritual fascinated me far more than the topic of his soliloquy. Standing next to his Adirondack chair, which overlooked the beach and broad expanse of lake, was a six-foot wooden crescent-shaped trough lined with tinfoil. From both sides of the middle of this trough protruded two arms which converged about four feet out from the belly of the crescent. Where the arms converged was a wire coat hanger, which was bent and folded to hold a flat, black Prince Albert pipe tobacco can filled with lake water. The whole contraption swiveled on a wooden base, so Mr. Irving could position the trough directly into the sun. As he proceeded to do just that, he said something about parabolas and focused sun's rays being like a magnifying glass, and ancient Greeks burning ships at sea. And it was all Greek to me, but by the time his explication ended, the tea water was boiling.

With a pair of pliers he poured the boiling water into a once white café-style mug, in which floated a Salada tea bag. The tea bag would be reused a couple more times before it was consigned to the compost bin.

After our fish foraging expedition, my hands smelled of dead fish. He told me to take my swim and get cleaned up. Anticipating this outcome, I had worn my bathing suit under my dungarees. While solidly ensconced in his chair, he sipped his tea and puffed on his pipe and kept an eagle eye on me, without letting on he was doing so.

When it was time to head back to camp for lunch, I did so carrying my shirt laden with yellow squash, radishes, and green beans. I noticed that the watermelons, which had been an enormous success, were not offered.

I remember an occasion when I visited Mr. Irving on a fall afternoon. I had been in school just a few weeks and my grandparents and I had come to camp for the weekend. My grandfather liked being at Camp best at that time of year because the "summer folk" closed and locked up their summer homes and returned to their full-time endeavors, leaving the lake quiet and solitary, and us feeling rather like pioneers in the wilderness. At least that was my fantasy.

Mr. Irving greeted me as though I left just that morning. He put aside his reading, and as we chatted, I noted with prepubescent male interest his gun rack on the wall. I had looked at it several times in the past and wanted to ask him about his guns, and hunting and shooting in general, but I never thought of a way to ask without appearing woefully ignorant and totally bereft of what many of my peers considered to be one of the basic rudiments of young manly knowledge. Horse and carriage, pie and ice cream, boys and guns: some things go naturally together, two matched halves making a whole, and somehow my other half had never materialized.

In his inimitable fashion, Mr. Irving decided that the time had come rectify my deficiencies in that area and casually asked if I might like to try my hand at target practice. He selected a .22 caliber rifle, a box of ammunition, and we adjourned to his porch, which overlooked his boathouse and part of the lake. Along the way, he retrieved an empty can of Carnation condensed milk and some toilet paper. He stuffed toilet paper into the can's opening and told me to go down to the seawall and throw the can as far out onto the lake as I could.

Upon my return to the porch, I commented that the distance was so great I could barely see the can. His laconic reply was that if I could see it then I could shoot it. Thus ensued an explanation of aiming, sight elevation, trajectory decline over distance, windage, and so on. And all I wanted to do was shoot. Nothing was ever simple with Mr. Irving - except our friendship.

He demonstrated how the rifle should be held and passed it to me. I eagerly seized it and promptly almost dropped it. I couldn't believe how heavy it was. My scrawny arms could not hold the rifle in position for more than a few seconds before its weight and gravity inexorably forced the muzzle downwards.

I think I heard a muffled chuckle as Mr. Irving gracefully intervened and propped the rifle on the porch railing. There was some comment made about there always being more than one way to skin a cat, whatever that meant. Then I fired…and fired…and fired. It took almost the entire box of ammunition before I sank the can, but sink it I did. Subsequent weekends showed progress.

Twelve years later, on the firing range at Fort Dix, I qualified as expert with the M-14 and I remembered little empty Carnation cans and Mr. Irving … and I silently saluted him.

LADY SLIPPERS

Grandma loved flowers. She loved their varied hues, the delicacy of their petals, and the uniqueness of each and every fragrance. During the blooming seasons her house in Concord had an artfully displayed assortment of flowers in various vases, decanters, and Mason jars—on the dining room table, the living room, and in the bathroom. When at Camp, lady slippers graced the table. In the early Spring she was seen burying her substantial nose in a small handheld bouquet of daffodils and in late Spring her nose was in a vase of lilac clumps. Occasionally I queried her as to the provenance of the pollen smudge on her nose.

Often, upon a late summer's afternoon at Camp, she would demand that we take a quick trip around the lake to see what was up. What this meant in translation was she wanted to see who had planted what in their flower beds and what was in full efflorescence at the moment. Grandpa would patiently slow the car down as we approached a cottage bedecked with flower pots, flowerbeds, and flowered window boxes, and Grandma, ensconced in the safety of the old Ford, would peer out the side window, scrutinizing from a safe distance every bloom and petal. This surveillance was accompanied by a running commentary comparing this year's display with last year's, the flowers of this house with those of the cottage just passed, and why on earth did they ever place jonquils next to geraniums, or irises in front of lilies. Grandpa and I understood these were merely rhetorical questions, serving solely as a springboard for Grandma's opinions, of which she had an abundance.

While Grandma loved flowers, she, unlike the quintessential earth mother who loved all her children equally, loved one particular flower above all others: the pink lady slipper - and the pink lady slipper grew in several hemlock-shaded areas about the Camp. Mr. Irving once told her that lady slippers also known as the moccasin flower, were a type of wild orchid and came in white, yellow, and pink. He said that taxonomically they were known as *Cypripedium Acaule,* which at her request, he wrote down for her. She had visions of showing off her new knowledge to various friends and relatives. Fortunately, she lost the scrap of paper. As Grandpa champed at the bit awaiting the spring ice-out, which signaled the opening of Camp, Grandma impatiently awaited the emergence of these fragile and relatively rare beauties.

Her house in Concord sported two ancient clumps of lilac trees; one was located directly front and center of her house and set back from the sidewalk. The second clump was located at the rear of her house and guarded the ramp into the barn. These two clumps would bloom in late May and the house and immediate environs became redolent with lilac's sweet perfume. As she directed Grandpa in the annual pruning of their sucker branches, she voiced her perennial complaint that she was stuck with the white variety of lilac instead of the purple. She claimed the white variety wasn't as long-lasting as the purple and when the white passed their prime the brown blotches of dying and decay were unsightly, whereas the purple simply faded gracefully away. However often she uttered this displeasure, she never progressed beyond veleity and took the next step to have Grandpa cut down the old clumps and replant them with the more desirable purple. A dense bed of Lilies of the Valley bordered the street side of her house.

* * *

Mamie, my great grandmother, had a chronic hip problem which caused her much discomfort, a state, which my Grandpa believed, and occasionally muttered under his breath, that she was all too willing to share with those around her. She usually walked in slow, shuffling, tentative steps. Sometimes she chose to use a pair of crutches when her pain levels were on the rise. When her pangs became too great, a condition she attributed to rising barometric pressure - a climatologically feature she checked several times a day by examining the rise and fall of colored water in a glass vial attached to the kitchen window frame - she took to her bed - a matriclinal response Grandma also utilized with her "sick headaches" and moments of pique.

Fortunately, Bristol was home to Calley and Currier, a crutch manufacturer, who produced and sent crutches all over the world. They also maintained a retail outlet locally and it was here that Mamie came to purchase her canes, crutches, and rubber replacement tips. Just a few doors down the street was Edward D. Crosby and Company, a manufacturer of croquet sets, ten pins, and chair stock. One day, while accompanying Mamie in her quest for crutch tips, Junior, in passing Crosby's store front, spied a shiny, new croquet set on display. He had been reading *The Great Gatsby* and suffered from yearnings for pharaonic wealth, sybaritic revelries, and lavish lawn parties at which elegantly clad young men and women of privilege played badminton and croquet. In an instant Junior knew he had to have a croquet set... Later, that same day, Uncle Bob was busily pressing wickets into the rocky ground behind the Camp as Junior officiously pointed out placement spots while reading aloud the rules and regulations of the game. At Junior's behest, Grandpa and Grandma were pressed into service for the Camp's first tournament. Somehow an attitude of anticipation and excitement infected them all.

Initially, it was thought gracious that Junior encouraged everyone to go ahead of him - until he began to pick them off one by one from behind. He whacked Uncle Bob's ball in a line drive toward the outhouse. It careened off a frost-heaved boulder, ricocheted off a swamp maple, and stopped in the middle of a blackberry patch. Grandpa's ball went barreling towards the boat dock and straight into the lake. Grandpa's frosty glare adequately indicated his displeasure and Grandma querulously stated that she didn't think that was how the game should be played. Caught up in a croquet equivalent of blood-lust, Junior was oblivious to the growing antipathy around him. With needless truculence he slammed Grandma's ball into a hemlock tree and like a bowling ball scattering ten pins, he thoroughly flattened a charming little group of three pink lady slippers, rendering their slender green stalks bent and broken, their thumb-sized pink pouches flattened in the earth.

A horrified gasp from Grandma rent the air, followed by dead silence. Then, "That will be enough of that. You can put that game of yours right back in its box and take it home. I don't want to see it here again." She went to the crushed lady slippers and ponderously knelt down, lovingly touching them. There was no hope of resurrection. She snipped the stalks with her fingernails and clambered herself upright. Slowly, she made her way inside the Camp, cradling the ravaged flowers in her hands, as one might a wounded bird. The porch door closed quietly behind her.

* * *

To the rear of her house in Concord was a double-lot wide backyard with a flat lawn in which

Junior's croquet game enjoyed a revival. He and
Uncle Bob played badminton and croquet with
friends and neighbors on summer evenings until it
was too dark to see. Convivial tournaments were
held on Thursday nights, the highlight of which was
homemade ice cream. The losing team had to crank
the handle of the iced cream tub. Grandma
occasionally watched the badminton games, but
pointedly ignored the croquet games; however,
whenever the homemade ice cream appeared, so did
she.

* * *

America joined the war in Europe, which soon
became the cynosure of attention and conversation
on the home front. Uncle Bob wanted to enlist and
Junior was dating Lena, my mother-to-be, and
pontificating in his typical oppositional manner
about the morality of the Conscientious Objector
position.

Patriotism was "*de rigueur*," anything less was
regarded with askance. Grandma let Junior know
that his philosophical rants were not welcome, were
tantamount to subversion, and he had best not
embarrass the family any further. At least his
brother had his head on straight. Junior was stung
by Grandma's words and lack of support. While
licking his wounds, he married my mother and
shortly thereafter she was with child - me.

Grandma had another "chat" with Junior,

informing him that while a wife and child might defer him from the draft in the eyes of the Selective Service Board, it did not excuse him in her eyes and he had best rectify his situation immediately, if not sooner. He joined the Merchant Marines before the week was out.

Junior returned home on leave from the Sheepshead Bay Maritime Training Academy a cook-in-training. Grandma pitched a fit: a common cook was totally unacceptable. Being in the Merchant Marines was bad enough (it wasn't the military), but it was better than being a Conscientious Objector. But a cook? Any Tom, Dick, or Harry could be a cook. When he returned to the academy, he became a radio operator and later earned the rank of Warrant Officer. My mother once said, whimsically, "But he did learn to make a really nice pie…and what can you do with all that Morse code stuff?"

With the boys off to war, the croquet and badminton sets found a new home in the attic.

* * *

Victory gardens became the fashion. Grandma didn't have one. When yet another neighbor was observed breaking ground for his garden, Grandma, ever conscious of social approbation as well as its animadversions, began to feel uncomfortable. There was no doubting her patriotism - Mamie had thoroughly inculcated that value. Her dilemma was simple: as much as she loved flowers, she did not like gardening. She didn't like being on her knees, didn't like to perspire, didn't like dirt - especially under her fingernails - didn't like being out in the sun, detested worms, insects in general and spiders in particular. The sight of a snake would drive her up a tree, as if one could imagine Grandma's rotund body scrabbling up a pine tree.

She received a letter from Junior. He was in port in Cairo and extolled the sights of Egypt. The pyramids were spectacular and the sphinx enigmatic. There was some sort of fracas with a camel and the camel bit him. The details were either unclear or missing, but I guess the camel survived. He missed everyone and when he came home on leave next he couldn't wait to beat the pants off his brother at croquet. That was what tipped the balance vis-à-vis Grandma's Victory Garden dilemma: she would have one after all, right in the middle of the back yard where the croquet game was situated during the summer months. Grandpa could dig it, plant it, weed it, and harvest it. She would work right along with him, giving supervision every step of the way. A nice border of pansies, she thought, would be pretty.

The vegetable garden did well. So did the pansies. Thus encouraged, Grandma had Grandpa dig up a couple of clumps of lady slippers at Camp. She carefully nestled their roots in wet newspaper for the return trek to Concord. Immediately upon arrival, Grandpa bustled them to the back yard and planted them in a newly dug extension of the pansy border. He watered them faithfully every day. Every day they appeared more spindly, their pink pouches losing color, looking washed out, their cernous heads drooping lower and lower. They struggled for a week and-a-half and then, gray and wilted, they keeled over and flopped flat on the ground. I think the lady slippers gave up the moment they left the Camp.

Shortly thereafter, the State of New Hampshire began a promotional program to protect the pink lady slipper. While it was not officially endangered, it was declared illegal to pick or transplant them. They were also designated as the state flower. Everyone wondered how Grandma would react to this news. Would she continue to grace the Camp's dining room table with their fragile beauty or would she heed the admonitions of the state? She was well-known for her stubbornness, but she also had a healthy respect for things governmental - again inculcated by her mother, Mamie. It was a fifty-fifty bet...and those who placed their bets on Grandma's compliance would have won.

* * *

It was Fall and the summer crowd had gone home. The lake was silent and serene, the sky a cerulean blue with that knife-edge clarity that heightens the senses and almost hurts the eyes. Everything in sight took on a deeper depth, as though the lake's ambit had magnified its third dimension. We were closing the Camp for the season. Grandpa came inside from some busywork out by the bay window that overlooked the horseshoe pit and part of the backyard. He asked Grandma to accompany him outside, he wanted to show her something. Normally she was not someone to interrupt; usually others waited on her to finish whatever she was doing before bravely venturing a suggestion or question. However, on that day, for whatever inexplicable reason, Grandma willingly left what she was doing and followed Grandpa outside. He led her to the back corner of the Camp by the bay window, a spot that caught the early morning's sun, where in the middle of a three-foot circle of newly dug up earth stood a clump of three, seven-foot saplings. A white envelope hung from the main stem of one of them. Grandpa detached the envelope and presented it to Grandma. She opened it. Inside was a cream-colored, heavy weight card upon which were engraved the words: "In loving celebration of our wedding anniversary." There was another piece of paper inside the envelope. It was a tag from a nursery in Bristol proclaiming the saplings to be genuine, imported French Purple Lilacs.

THE COVE

A segment of that magnificent mural on the ceiling of the Sistine Chapel portrays two iconic figures - God and Adam - arms outstretched, forefingers pointing, almost touching. Those two fingers rivet the attention, the tiny space between them like the synaptic cleft breathlessly awaiting the explosive, heavenly connection.

That finger of land which gently rose from the lake bed and upon which my great-grandfather built the Camp was like one of those fingers-- wondrous and magical. The cove was a deep crescent indentation just back from the land's fingertip and along its southeastern flank the morning sun would flood its soft golden warmth, slowly dissipating the silvery-gray mist that hovered over the water's tranquil surface, often revealing that motionless sentry, the Great Heron that fished there.

Often I awoke early on a Sunday morning. I'd lie in my bed, not stirring and listen to the quiet sounds of the nascent breaking day-- birds calling each other, my grandfather grinding his teeth in the adjoining bedroom, and the occasional distant drone of an outboard motor taking a dedicated fisherman to a favorite spot.

Dressing noiselessly, I'd tiptoe out of my bedroom, pulling aside the heavy green curtain that served as a door, and creep downstairs to the living room and then into the dining room. Early sunlight shafted through the window behind the table, highlighting the big glass ashtray heaped with the butts of Grandpa's Camels. When he got up in a little while, he'd empty them in the cast iron Glenwood. Then he'd light a fire to take the chill off.

Passing through the kitchen I'd smell the distinctive odor of the kitchen's kerosene stove, which was my job to keep filled, and carefully open the door to the porch. This door had a chronic hinge-squawk half-way through its opening. I had discovered that if I lifted up on the handle and opened the door quickly the squawk was softer and shorter-lived than if I tried to open it slowly.

Through the screened-in porch, down the steps, and along the laid stone walkway to the backyard I'd scurry until about ten feet from the boat landing, I'd slow down and proceed carefully and deliberately until I reached the opening in the trees that framed the boat dock. I'd sit down on my butt and slowly scooch forward a couple feet until I could see down the length of the cove to the Little Frog Pond where the sentry usually stood guard. Sure enough, there he was, sometimes standing on one leg, sometimes on both, but always stock still and staring directly at me.

I often wondered which one of us was anticipating the presence of the other. We stared at each other, quiet and unmoving, the tendrils of white mist swaying and drifting upwards until disappearing in the morning sunlight. His beady eyes implacable and inscrutable, mine wide with wonder. Sometimes the Great Heron, after several long seconds of assessment, would disdainfully launch himself into the air. His huge wings slowly flapped to lift his imponderable body, its giraffe-like neck outstretched, to tree-top level, and then languidly glide around the corner to the next cove.

Other times the Great Heron ignored me as though I was as insignificant as just another stone on that rock-strewn shoreline. At these times I think he was in hunting mode because he'd stare into the water statue-like, his long neck coiled into an S shape. He reminded me of a feathered snake ready to strike. Suddenly, he would, too fast for the eye to follow, his long beak emerged from the shallow lake water with a frog or sometimes a yellow perch or rock bass. He never ate in front of me, but always slowly flapped his way around the same pine-studded corner and vanished from my sight.

I imagined we had a special kind of trans-species relationship. On those mornings that I woke up early and crept out to see him, I believed he was waiting for me to appear. Maybe he wondered about me as I wondered about him. A few times when Grandpa and I drove past the Big Frog Pond to get the Sunday paper, I saw the Great Heron knee-deep in water thick with lily pads and eelgrass and coiled in hunting mode, I felt the first pangs of prepubescent betrayal. Why was he here and not in our cove where he belonged?

*   *   *

There came a spring when we came to Camp much earlier than usual, just a few days after ice-out. The day was bright and sunny, the air warm, a harbinger of even warmer days to come. We aired the place out to make it ready for summer use, I discovered that Junior had left his fiberglass kayak in storage under the camp. We dusted and swept and took sheets off furniture and beds, I found myself thinking more and more of that kayak, the sunny day, and the sparkling waters of the cove. They beckoned.

It didn't take long before I decided it was time for a break from my labors and go for a short spin. Because the water was still freezing cold and I didn't have a wet suit, I decided to stay in the cove in case the unthinkable happened and I flipped over and had to swim. I figured I could make it to the closest shore before hyperthermia overtook me. As I write this I remember a phrase Mr. Irving used in my presence. It was something about "the arrogance of the young...."

I dragged Junior's red and white kayak out from under the Camp and dusted it off. The double-bladed paddle was stowed in the cockpit. There was no sign of a spray skirt and I didn't know if he even had one, but then he wasn't a whitewater kind of guy anyway. I hefted the boat onto my right shoulder, paddle in my other hand, and eagerly trotted to the boat landing.

Dropping the paddle, I lowered the kayak to the

ground and slid it into the water. I slithered myself into the cockpit by taking a paddle brace off a flat rock at the water's edge and dipped my hand in the water just to see. *Jeez it was cold.*

I paddled slowly along the left shoreline, past the blueberry bushes, enjoying the sun on my face and the sensory pleasure of muscles once again falling into the old familiar routine of dip, push-pull, lift and rotate wrist, and repeat on the other side. I coasted to the belly of the cove, past the Little Frog Pond's entrance and the Great Heron's early morning feeding ground and turned up the other eastern side of the cove. I noticed something strange. The water's surface was riffling, but there was no wind. Suddenly I realized that all around me, in fact fully half of the cove was stirred up with tiny splashes and swirls of miniature currents, but there was no wind. I looked down into the water and almost dropped my paddle. The water was filled with millions of fish: yellow perch. The water was thick with them. Each careful paddle stroke was a shovel full of fish. They appeared to have no direction or pattern, just constantly milling about. I couldn't see how deep the mass of writhing fish bodies extended down they were so densely packed - like the proverbial sardines in a can.

I paddled carefully and slowly to the center of the cove. I didn't want to injure any of them with the paddle blade. As suddenly as I had entered this teeming mass I crossed a line of demarcation and they were no more—like there was some invisible boundary line that kept them penned up in that half of the cove.

So amazed was I at this phenomenon that I turned the kayak around and reentered the swirling, milling mass of fish again, just to be sure that what I had witnessed was in fact real. It was.

As I came ashore I chuckled thinking of the Sentry, the Great Heron, and what he would have thought of this. Dinners for many lifetimes. I wonder if he would ponder this amazing event or if he would have simply and pragmatically begun spearing a meal.

*   *   *

Deep in the back of the cove there is a small space between the rocks where a small boat, like a rowboat or canoe can pass through. This is the entrance to the Little Frog Pond where the Sentry, or Great Heron, often spends his early mornings. Beyond the entrance the area fans out in an elliptical shape, perhaps a hundred feet by forty. The water is shallow, ranging from ten inches to two feet. There are lily pads, a few small rocks for turtles to sun themselves on, and there used to be a ton of frogs. Not so many these days. Their near annihilation will be recounted here.

Family legend offers the following—Junior wanted to go to college. To go to a liberal arts college in those days, one had to have a couple years of a language, typically French or German.

Junior chose the former. Sometime along in his coursework the French teacher talked a bit about French cuisine. The teacher's remarks about escargot and frogs legs caught Junior's attention. Sometime later, while at Camp, the idea struck him that the family should be exposed to this delicacy, and there was the Frog pond just sitting there, a veritable warehouse of potential gourmet dining. He persuaded his younger brother to join him in this venture, not a difficult task because Uncle Bob looked up to Junior and almost always went along with his schemes.

The next step was to persuade Grandma to go along with the idea because it would be up to her to do the cooking. Neither boy cooked, nor ever intended to. Persuading Grandma wasn't as difficult as one might think because Junior had been manipulating her all his life and knew her soft spots and obstinacies like the back of his hand. He used a two-pronged attack, which he later had the bad manners to brag about. First, he would appeal to her pride in him as a superior student by claiming this experiment in frog leg dining was a project for extra credit in his French class. Second, he appealed to her vanity as one of the better families in town because only the elite would have the style and good breeding to make the effort to become acquainted with the esteemed viands of other civilized cultures. Yup, she bought it. I think Grandpa probably rolled his eyes. He was a beans and franks kind of guy and he'd seen Junior at work before. The event was planned for the following weekend at Camp.

Grandma was instructed to check her cookbooks for recipes and Junior and Uncle Bob busily got to work making spears. Junior claimed the proper term for these spears was "leisters," although no one but him had ever heard of the term. Somehow Junior had gotten it into his head that the only way to procure the raw product, frogs, was to spear them. He and Uncle Bob spent a while thrashing about the woods sawing and hacking branches, trimming them, and finally fashioning what to Junior's eye were acceptable spear ("leister") shafts. "Borrowed" forks from the kitchen were lashed with string to the ends of these shafts to complete the frog-spearing tridents. There was some frustration expressed by Junior that there was no way to put barbs on the fork tines. Its funny what some people get compulsive about. Soon after the great frog hunt began.

They took the old rowboat, the very one that a few years later they were to run aground upon a reef, and made their way down the cove to the Little Frog Pond. They rowed through the entrance, shipped oars, and commenced to slaughter, to wreak havoc and carnage upon the unsuspecting amphibian population. Spears flew, kitchen forks impaled, tines jabbed, and entrails soon smeared the bottom of the boat. Reboant shrieks and yells of battle filled the air: "There's one…over there…get em…don't let him get away…you missed him…."

Family legend has it that untold numbers of frogs were "harvested" during that memorable event and the resultant "mess" in the rowboat of dead frogs, frog parts, guts and gore was unimaginable. When it was time to dissect the legs from the frogs, the blood-lust of battle, the hunting frenzy seemed to have dissipated and was quickly replaced by certain feelings of repugnance and squeamishness.

I'm told they never ate a single frog leg. I don't know what happened to the mound of dead and dying frogs. I do know that the predictable nocturnal cacophony of bull frog croaks and accompanying amphibian din was greatly reduced for years afterwards. And I expect that Grandpa, much to his relief, probably dined on beans and franks that night.

* * *

My earliest recollection of being on a boat on the lake was when I was perhaps five or six years old. The Camp had a beat up and battered old wooden rowboat that Junior and Uncle Bob thoroughly abused during their youth. On this particular occasion they had resurrected an ancient outboard motor, clamped it on the rowboat's stern, and engaged in the dubious process of persuading my grandma to go for a spin. I say dubious because Grandma didn't really like being in the water, never mind being on top of it. Who knew what dangers lurked below in those dark depths.

The begging and pleading, teasing and cajoling

went on for a while and eventually, to my surprise Grandma finally relented and agreed to go - just in the cove. I say surprised because while Grandma usually succumbed to Junior's wheedling and temper tantrums, her fear of the water was on a par with her fear of thunder, lightning, and fire. She hardly ever confronted those fears, and what motivated her this time remains a puzzle to me. What also motivated her to accompany Grandpa on those twilight excursions in Mr. Irving's White Ghost baffles me as well. Perhaps the size of his boat made a difference as well as a reluctance to expose a weakness to anyone outside the family.

I remember it was a commotion getting Grandma aboard that rickety old boat. Grandma and Grandpa were the quintessential Jack Sprat and wife. He was skinny as a rail and she was large. She was not only large, but like many large people she was ungainly on her feet, not well coordinated, and had little sense of balance. Also, like most women of that time, she always wore a dress or skirt. Pants on a woman was unthinkable.

Uncle Bob was waist-deep in the water holding the boat parallel to the rocky shore. Junior held Grandma's arm as she unsteadily clambered over the rocks to the side of the boat. She put one foot on the gunwale with the intent of stepping from the side of the boat down to the seat and then down to the floorboard, thence to sit on the bow seat. That was the plan anyway. Grandma put her weight on her foot. The side of the rowboat sank almost to water level.

"Oh dear," Grandma gasped as she lurched back, clutching Junior's arm to steady herself. Junior, unprepared for this sudden weight shift on his arm staggered as he struggled to regain his balance and not let go of Grandma. Meanwhile the rowboat rocked back, causing a substantial wave of compressed water to thoroughly drench Uncle Bob. I thought it was great fun.

Evidently Grandma wasn't going to be able to board the boat in that manner. Uncle Bob simply could not hold the boat level with her weight on the opposite side. Grandma was ready to call it quits for the day. Junior wasn't. His next plan, hurriedly and glibly stated, was to turn the boat around and place its stern next to a large rock so Grandma could just step from the rock onto the stern seat and then to the floorboards. This plan worked.

The next thing I remember is all of us in the boat: Junior, Uncle Bob, Grandma, and me, and the boat drifting while Junior yanked on the outboard motor's starter rope…and yanked…and yanked. This went on for a while with an occasional snort from the motor, and Junior becoming redder in the face, and his yanks on the rope more vicious. Uncle Bob was studiously examining the slowly passing shore line and Grandma was making soothing noises at Junior, saying we could always try again tomorrow, that it was an old motor and none of this was his fault and he shouldn't get so worked up, which, of course, was exactly the wrong thing to say to him.

Suddenly the engine caught with a roar, a great belch of noxious, blue-gray smoke erupted into the air, and the rowboat surged forward, throwing us all off balance and Junior almost overboard. He wildly grabbed for the motor's steering arm as he fell sprawling half on the stern seat, half on the floor. Grandma made little whimpering noises as she clutched me in a crushing embrace, whether to protect me or just to hold on to something solid, I don't know. That derelict of a rowboat caroomed off one of its own waves and altered direction, heading directly for Mr. Chilton's Chris Craft, which placidly lay moored on the other side of the cove.

About a hundred feet beyond Mr. Chilton's mooring was a small reef, a cluster of erratics, or huge boulders that the glaciers had dropped thousands of years ago. They rose from the floor of the cove to just inches below the surface, depending on the time of year and water level. The New Hampshire Department of Fish and Game marked the area with two red-painted, warning buoys shortly after ice-out.

Junior picked himself up from the floor of the rowboat only to see Mr. Chilton's Chris Craft looming directly ahead, the distance closing at a sickening rate. He yanked the steering arm, the rowboat banked into its turn, narrowly missing the Chris Craft and a scarce couple seconds later crunched solidly onto the reef. Once again, everyone was thrown off balance and off their seats by the abrupt stop. The engine sputtered, hiccupped, and died.

A silence fell over the cove…and then a faint gurgle of water was heard. The floorboards began to move. Then they were floating… then bobbing up and down as the boat settled in the water. Uncle Bob jumped overboard to lighten the load. Junior followed out of self-preservation, leaving me and Grandma (an act never forgotten by us). She whimpered louder, clutched me tighter, and believing that one of her worst fears was about to be realized—drowning, she prepared to meet her maker.

All motion stopped. The boat had wedged itself among three of those huge boulders and was solidly suspended. There remained only a few inches of freeboard and the first wave from a passing boat would completely swamp it, but we would sink no farther. It took Grandma awhile to accept she was not going to drown after all and her whimpering moans of fright gradually subsided.

Mr. Chilton, roused from his afternoon nap by all the commotion, soon appeared on shore. It didn't take him long to bring his rowboat to our rescue. The trickiest part was transferring Grandma from our rowboat to his and preserving her modesty at the same time. Again, it was that business about wearing a dress. When we finally returned to Camp Grandma announced she was retiring to bed with a migraine.

*   *   *

I wanted to take the rowboat out on the lake myself. Grandma and Grandpa wouldn't let me. I had rowed Junior, my uncle, and Grandpa all around the southern third of the lake, around the island, and around the Point to the sandy beach by Mr. Irving's place. They still wouldn't let me row alone. They were adamant. I understood Grandma's reluctance: she was deathly afraid of drowning and her last time in a rowboat had almost ended in her demise, or so she believed and so frequently stated. I didn't understand my Grandpa's reluctance and it was only after repeated questioning did he, and with some embarrassment and quiet dignity, tell me the cause of his trepidation. He was afraid of drowning too. But it was not like Grandma's fear; his was the fear for others and the unexpected. He proceeded to explain.

When he was a young man he was charged with the care of three younger boys. They had all decided to go swimming. Grandpa was unfamiliar with the swimming hole the boys led him to. They told him it was their favorite place and they had swum there hundreds of times. There was a place for diving into the water. One of the boys dove in and never came up. Grandpa went in after him and found him trapped under some branches that had been caught between rocks. Grandpa never forgave himself for not having checked beneath the water before he allowed them to dive there. He never enjoyed swimming after that nor did he enjoy being in boats. He forced himself to swim in the cove periodically only to prove to himself he could still swim if he had to. His excursions in the rowboat with me were truly a labor of love. I never knew until then of his discomfort and courage.

Eventually they came around, of course, but it came with the condition that when I could swim across the wide mouth of the cove, then I could row the boat there. Naturally I tried to persuade them that if I ever did tip over that I'd never have to swim more than half the distance. They didn't buy it and stuck to their position. It was the whole distance or nothing.

Now I had never been a strong swimmer. As much as I loved the water and boats, I never became proficient at swimming. Oh, I could paddle about, side stroke, crawl, breast stroke, tread water, and float. I could make it out to the raft, but I had never been interested in distance. So I began, out to the raft and back. Again, and yet again. I think Grandpa got a kick out of it. He would come out to watch me. He seldom missed a "training session" as I had taken to calling it. He seldom said much, just watched. Once he commented, "You're making progress, lad." Grandma ignored the whole process.

I don't remember how long it took me to get to the point where I was sure I could do it, certainly less than half that summer. But the day did come when I asked Grandpa to row the boat behind me as I struck out for the opposite shore. I did the sidestroke the entire way since that was my strongest stroke. I took my time. I could hear Grandpa working the oars behind me. He never said a word, nor did I. When I got close enough so my feet could touch bottom, I stood up and waded in until I was knee deep and waited for Grandpa to glide up. With a small smile on his face, he said, "Pull the boat up, lad, so I can get out without getting my shoes wet. I'm walking home and you're rowing." He got out, clapped me on the shoulder, and walked off. And that was that.

REPAIRING ROAD

It is commonly accepted that the growth and expansion of any civilization depends in large part on its infrastructure, particularly its roads and bridges. Without good roads and bridges the transportation of goods and services, trade and military deployment are restricted and thus, the economic and military viability of a culture is stultified. Ancient Rome could not have conquered most of the known world without its famous roads, upon which its legendary legions marched throughout its sprawling empire. More to home, when General Eisenhower saw Germany's Autobahn, he immediately grasped its ramifications and applicability to military purposes, and thus our Interstate Highway System was born.

For a moment, consider the vitiating effects on the economic growth of China, Russia, and Asia if there had been no Silk Road, no Trans-Siberian Highway, and no Orient Express. Think of the debilitating effects on the economies and progress of London, San Francisco, and St. Petersburg if there were no London Bridge, no Golden Gate Bridge, and no Skyway Bridge. Think how the opening of America's western territory was aided by the Chisholm Trail, the Oregon Trail, the Boseman Trail, or the Wilderness Trail.

Accessibility to Alaska and Canada's Northwest Territories was greatly enhanced by the Trans-Alaska Highway. Some say speed hastens progress; others might debate the definition of "progress."

* * *

To get to Camp one turns off the paved secondary road of Star Route 3A onto an unmarked dirt road, a dirt road originally made for horse and wagon and scarcely improved since its creation. The advent of the automobile brought the need for occasional repair and little else, and more about that soon.

It was a narrow, one lane, winding, hill-climbing, hairpin-turning, pot holed, rutted challenge with few places to pull off if you met someone coming the other way. A large part of the mystery and magic of Camp for me was the difficulty in getting to and from it.

It was a road for strolling, for communing with Nature, for keeping the Sunday drivers out and the casual visitor from visiting. I loved it. Grandpa respected it. Grandma was indifferent.

As I said, to get to Camp, one turned off the secondary road on to the unmarked, dusty Camp road. On the left was a small field that usually yielded two cuttings of the sweetest smelling hay in the Northeast. For several days following a mowing the air was redolent with the wonderful aroma of that yellow harvest.

Beyond the field the dirt road became an isthmus, squeezed on the left by the Big Frog Pond and on the right by the Beach that Mr. Irving and I prowled in the mornings. On occasion, following a hard winter of record snowfall and a spring of several consecutive warm days, the snow melt caused flooding and the Big Frog Pond united with the Beach and covered the road with water, creating an island. The idea of the entire point becoming an island appealed to me greatly as a young boy. It reminded me of a picture I had seen in my French book of Mont-St. Michel.

The isthmus ended at the foot of a steep scrub-clad hill and the road abruptly turned ninety degree angles to the left and to the right. A sign post dead ahead designated which direction to go to find what camp. This area was called the Gate. I don't know why it was called the Gate or if there ever was a gate there. Our Camp lay to the left.

The road bordered the Big Frog Pond for about a thousand feet on the left. The hillside rose on the right. During the spring and early summer months this was an especially bad spot for mosquitoes. Half-way along this section was a small sandpit hidden by juniper bushes and young pine trees. We used the pit for road repair. Measuring a dozen feet across and four feet deep, it was a great place for young boys to hide and surreptitiously watch as the infrequent car drove by—or perhaps a Roman chariot or enemy patrol or a Conestoga wagon headed west.

The camp road rose up a short, steep hill, at the top of which another sand pit lay off to the right and not so well hidden. On the left towered a rampike, a giant white pine that had been split by lightning years ago, its splintered wood curiously streaked by black char and aged silvery-white. The road wiggled on the level for a bit then descended to a junction, dividing right, left, and straight ahead into a cottage's hemlock-covered driveway.

The road to Camp bore right, up another short, steep hill, at the top of which scrub brush concealed another sand pit. The road descended with a moderate grade passing the Little Frog Pond on the left - the scene of Junior and Uncle Bob's frog massacre. A sharp left following the shoreline of the Cove brings one into the oval-shaped driveway in front of the barn red, rambling, two-story structure of the Camp.

The road just described ran a half-mile in length and every couple of years Grandpa, his friend of many years, Roy, myself, and sometimes Junior and Uncle Bob gathered together for a weekend of repairing this road. It began with Grandma preparing breakfast.

Grandma, like Uncle Bob, enjoyed the reputation of having a "healthy appetite." Unlike Uncle Bob, that did not apply to the breakfast meal. She preferred tea, with either toast or a doughnut. Grandpa liked instant coffee accompanied by a block of shredded wheat, over which he poured boiling water and promptly drained it. That and a doughnut or toast. However, if either Junior or Uncle Bob were present, she put on a spread of assorted cereals, eggs and bacon and melon. Grandma loved to cook for her sons, especially Uncle Bob. She would always cook more than enough so she could coax him into having second, third, or sometimes even fourth helpings, always saying she didn't want any leftovers. We all looked forward to Uncle Bob's presence as well - except sometimes I would have appreciated some of those leftovers.

After breakfast we assembled in front of the padlocked double doors that sealed the storage area under the Camp. Swinging wide those doors, Grandpa pointed to the various tools needed and we took turns fetching them: wheelbarrow, spades, mattocks, sledgehammer, crowbars, metal pails, a come-a-long winch, a thirty foot length of stout chain that I could barely carry, and five chunks of firewood.

Grandpa and Roy led the way, conferring about the day's projects: crowns leveled, potholes filled, ruts smoothed over, protruding edges of rocks either knocked off or the boulder dug out, and intruding tree limbs trimmed. Junior and Uncle Bob did their brotherly chatter. I pushed the wheelbarrow.

It was a beautiful summer's morning, the sun warm upon the skin in those brief stretches of road without a tree cover. In the shadows the cool of the evening lingered. When we came to the first hill by the Little Frog Pond, I soon discovered the wheelbarrow was too heavy for me to push up hill. It was the chains and I was still a scrawny little kid.

Everyone but me found it amusing. Uncle Bob gently punched me in the shoulder, took the handles from me and said, "It's past my turn anyway, Pardner."

Uncle Bob called me "Pardner" for as long as I remember. It stemmed from our often discussed plans that when I got older, he and I would go out West together and become cowboys. We'd work for some ranch, ride palomino horses, and sit by campfires at night eating beans and franks with johnnycake and drink coffee. I'd be old enough to drink coffee by then. I believed in this bucolic storyline far longer than I believed in Santa Claus and the Tooth Fairy.

*   *   *

At the top of the hill Grandpa and Roy found our first project: a rock in the crown of the road that frost heaves had pushed a few more inches above the surface, just enough to graze the transmission case of a car whose driver didn't know enough to pull to the side and avoid it. Roy joked about leaving it where it was as a way to discourage Sunday driver exploration, but Grandpa demurred. The rock was too rounded to knock off with the sledgehammer so we had to dig it out and fill in the hole. Fortunately, it wasn't a big rock and the sandpit was only a few yards away so fill for the resultant hole didn't have to be carried far.

As we descended the hill we could see from a

distance that the tire ruts had deepened over the past two years, thus elevating the middle of the road, or crown, to almost scrape the undercarriage of a car. Uncle Bob showed me how to use the mattocks to chop off the crown and spread the dirt and small stones into the ruts to create a level surface. It wasn't very hard work and you got to see the results of your labors quickly. The rest of the crew proceeded along the road to the next project. I continued to hack at the crown. I raised the mattocks high in the air and brought it down hard, like I was chopping wood, pick -end first. It dug into the crown. I yanked it back and forth to loosen the earth. The next swing was with the flat bladed end, which scooped out the earth into the rut. Then using the spade, I spread the earth and pebbles out evenly, filling in the rut. It was pleasant work. Birds chirped and sang in the distance. A chipmunk scurried across the road and behind a log, only to poke his head up to stare at me quizzically. In about an hour I had completed my twenty foot section and I went to join the others.

They were clustered at the junction where the road went left, right, and into a driveway. Just off-center of this junction the crew had dug around a large rock, whose exposed triangular pointed top caused every observant driver to swing wide to avoid it. What first appeared as a few inches of threat turned into a three-foot long, two-foot thick, several hundred -pound monster.

This was now a major project requiring digging

out around the rock so one could get at it and then digging a ramp to roll the rock up and out of the hole. Rolling entailed using the crowbars as levers and the chunks of firewood as blocks to prevent the rock from rolling back into the hole. This was backbreaking, dangerous work: fingers and hands, toes and feet could be mangled and crushed. I was told to keep out of the way and just watch. By watching I finally understood what Mr. Irving had told me about Archimedes' adage: given a lever long enough he could lift the world. Our crowbars weren't that long, but we had two of them - and Roy.

Roy was a bear of a man, taller than average, broad and thick. He reminded me of the first six-and-a-half feet of an oak tree. He smoked cigars. His voice was a basso profundo rumble to which he gave free rein in the church choir. I remember him singing the Lord's Prayer and my entire spine shivering with electricity when he rolled out the bass notes.

Roy loved physical work, especially road repair. He would attack an errant boulder like a hungry bear attacks a hollow log containing a honey hive: all rip and tear, push and shove, grunt and sweat. His white undershirt became soaked with perspiration and streaked with dirt almost before he began. For a man who didn't believe in cursing, he skirted the edges, "Gor ram it, you mothering bugger…you will move you're hairy backside, NOW!" as he heaved on a crowbar. The rock grudgingly budged an inch. I loved watching Roy.

Grandpa spoke out that if they could pry, push, or roll the boulder out of the hole plus two feet toward the side of the road, the chain and come-a-long winch attached to a nearby hemlock could reach it and move it the rest of the way. Roy and Junior redoubled their efforts with the crowbars. As the boulder was raised a few inches Uncle Bob would chock it with firewood chunks and other rocks. Pry and lever up, chock it, pry and lever up, chock it....Finally the boulder rolled over, yielding three feet of progress.

At this point we heard a car's engine approaching. We turned en mass toward the noise. Mr. Chilton's black ford came down the hill, slowly crawled over my newly leveled crowns and filled in ruts, and came to a stop. Mr. Chilton's angular frame emerged from his vehicle, the dappled sunlight glancing off his bald pate. He walked up to us and nodded approvingly as he surveyed the work area and said with a smile, "Well, I guess I didn't need to get to town so early after all. How long do you fellas think you'll be?"

Then commenced a meandering discussion of time estimates, other troublesome spots along the road, a new house being built on the main road, the weather lately, and a supper that the Congregational Church was putting on that night in town. Mr. Chilton, apparently in no hurry, finally returned to his Ford, started the engine, put it in reverse, and slowly backed up the hill the way he'd come.

At last the boulder was within reaching distance of the chain. Roy looped one end around the rock, the other to the come-a-long, which in turn had its steel cable wrapped around the trunk of an obliging hemlock. Roy cranked the come-a-long's handle taking up the slack until it was taut as a bowstring. Roy said if by chance he couldn't drag the boulder with the come-a-long then Junior and Uncle Bob would have to use their crowbars and pry in unison with Roy's efforts. They positioned themselves, crowbars jammed under the bottom edge of the rock, ready to put their weight on the bars. It wasn't necessary. Roy's muscular body appeared to expand to Bunyonesque proportions as he squeezed the come-a-long's handle to him. As the come-a-long's ratchet click- clicked, the chain made ominous, metallic creaking sounds; the length of it thrummed and quivered under the strain. The boulder slid several inches. Everyone cheered, except Roy, who was huffing and puffing and squeezing again. After that it was short work to drag the boulder to the side of the road where, with the aid of Junior and Uncle Bob's crowbars, they maneuvered it into place just off the edge of the road. It would have made a great safety barrier if there had been a drop-off behind, but there wasn't.

Now came the task of pushing the wheelbarrow to the sand pit, filling it with dirt and small stones and then returning to the gaping hole to fill it. My job was to dig up dirt and fill the metal pails, which in fire brigade fashion, Uncle Bob passed to Junior, who dumped it in the wheelbarrow. It took three wheelbarrow loads to fill that hole.

Grandpa declared it was time to break for lunch. Grandma had prepared it with Uncle Bob in mind. While in the Navy, my uncle had been introduced to Hormel's latest culinary blockbuster to grace the American palate - Spam. I'm told the U.S. Navy served a lot of it and Uncle Bob was a grateful recipient. He unabashedly loved the stuff. Consequently, whenever Grandma knew he was coming to visit, she would lay in several cans. On that day she had heated up a platter of sliced Spam, along with mashed potatoes and green beans. There was a plate stacked with slices of Wonder Bread in case he wanted to make Spam sandwiches to take with him after lunch to tide him over to supper.

Grandma had also made a pitcher of iced tea. Her iced tea was her summer trademark. She made it from scratch every morning during the summer months, whether she was at home or at Camp. She'd pour boiling water over Salada tea bags and let it steep. To that she'd add quartered lemons and scoops of white sugar. If I was nearby she'd have me stir and taste it. She always asked me if I thought it needed more sugar. Usually I said yes and she'd add more - a miniscule amount. Nonetheless, it made me feel important.

The conversation over lunch was usually between Junior and Grandma. Grandpa seldom interjected. Uncle Bob mostly ate. I cut my Spam into small Lincoln Log facsimiles and constructed miniature forts and houses. We always wound up waiting for Uncle Bob to finish his third or fourth helping that Grandma had pressed upon him.

After lunch we returned to retrieve the wheelbarrow of tools we had stowed behind a spruce tree and continued down the road. Roy pointed out a sharp blade of rock coming out from the sloping hillside on the left and angling down into the tire rut. There was enough room to swing a car out of its way, but Roy found that idea as offensive as the rock's location itself. With a gleam in his eye he reached for the sledgehammer and strode over to the rock. He raised his weapon high overhead and with both hands brought it down with a resounding CRUNK. A football-sized shard went flying off into the woods. Roy raised the sledge again, and once again a chunk of rock went ricocheting through the air. Most of the offending rock protrusion was demolished at this point and only a few more blows to blunt the resulting sharp edges were all that was needed to complete the job. Roy seemed quite satisfied with his work and with himself.

When we approached the Big Frog Pond, Grandpa pointed out how the swamp maples thrived in the low-lying wet areas. I remembered them being spectacularly beautiful the previous fall with their predominant reds, maroons, and scarlets reflecting their brilliance in the still water. However, their branches were extending into the road and Grandpa, ever concerned about the appearance of his vehicle, didn't want the chance of them scratching his car. He pruned those branches with a patient deliberateness.

I leveled a few more crowns that day. Roy pulverized a few more rocks. Junior and Uncle Bob dug out a few more boulders. I remember most the spirit of camaraderie we all shared, the easy, friendly banter, and the sharing of a task in service to the Camp.

Some years later one of the cottages changed ownership and the new owner was the proprietor of a small construction company, the kind that digs cellar holes and pushes dirt around. One overcast gray day he brought in a flatbed laden with a bulldozer to the turn-off from the secondary road. He unloaded it and began to bulldoze his way to his cottage, leveling crowns, filling in ruts, widening the road, smoothing the curves, and even carving out a few pull-over spots. Not long after that, some land was sold off, lots were divided, and shiny cottages with big plate glass windows and sliding glass doors opening onto decks appeared. A proper road had brought progress and nothing was the same - part of the magic had died.

THE BOAT HOUSE

Mr. Irving's boat house jutted out from his sea wall some twenty-five feet into the lake. It rested on huge boulders and two equally large concrete buttresses at the deeper end. Its board and batten walls were painted a pale yellow and white paint trimmed the eves and corner posts.

This boat house could be seen a mile away, a veritable beacon for boaters coming down the east side of the lake. Since his home was screened from public view by various conifers and shrubs, the blatant obviousness of this beacon was another paradox in this complex gentleman.

* * *

At a tick above idling speed, Mr. Irving's long, sleek motor launch, christened the "White Ghost," lined up dead center on the wide, gaping doors of his boat house and slowly glided into the dark, mysterious, slightly ominous interior. He cut the engine and the throaty shuga, shuga ceased. The silence became more pervasive as we drifted inside. I thought of Jonah and the Whale. Mr. Irving reached out in the dark with his boat hook, hit an unseen lever and suddenly the inside of the boat house was bathed in dim, rutilant light from a low wattage incandescent bulb. He was not one to waste money on superfluous illumination.

The boat sat quietly within an eight-foot-wide

U-shaped dock, which ringed the interior of the boat house. White stuffed canvas fenders prevented the boat from scraping its sides against the dock. Upon the walls hung various boating paraphernalia: coiled ropes, life jackets, extra fenders, cans of motor oil on wooden shelves, fishing poles leaning in one corner, a tackle box, and unlabeled cardboard boxes of various sizes were stuffed side by side on shelves. The sharp smell of gasoline mixed with sun-warmed, old wooden boards, and lake water hung in the air.

Mr. Irving heaved his bulk to his feet and with surprising surefootedness stepped up onto the starboard seat, which ran the length of the cockpit, and then up on the gunwale and onto the dock. He turned and held out a gnarly, callused hand to help me scramble out of the boat.

"Watch this," he said, "I think you'll get a kick out of it."

He walked along the dock to midship where a long chain hung in the air. He began to pull down on this chain, hand over hand. From the water, fore and aft under his boat, black, wet chains emerged, dripping with water and cradling the "White Ghost." As he continued to haul on the chain, the boat lurched slightly and rose from the surface to hang suspended three feet in the air.

Seeing my look of astonishment, Mr. Irving explained that when waves were running, whether caused by wind or other motorboats, they not only crashed on the shore, but they came rolling under the boat house doors as well. Even with the fenders out, his boat would sooner or later suffer wear and tear. Suspending his boat saved needless battering and subsequent repair. But in addition to the pragmatics, he thought it was fun to hoist all that weight and mass into the air with one hand. He went on about something called davits and laws of physics, blocks and tackles, pulleys and weight differentials over distance, levers, and some guy called Archimedes.

When he went on like that I usually didn't pay much attention, but I do remember staring at the "White Ghost" hanging in the air with lake water streaming down its sides and the effortless way he pulled it up out of the water. He seemed to me at that moment to be like Moses parting the Red Sea.

If I walked along the inside dock to the open doors and peered into the water, I usually could see minnows swimming about and sometimes a small rock bass or a shiner. The shade of the boat house attracted them. I hoped to see a fat, old, lake trout lolling in that water someday, but I never did. I didn't know much about lake trout.

In the front corner of the boat house, under the eaves, barn swallows had made their mud nest. Knowing Grandma's aversion to dirt, I thought I might be helpful and knock it down. I could wash off the mud by using his wooden step ladder. When I made my offer, I thought for a minute Mr. Irving was going to swallow his pipe. He got himself under control and hastened to set me straight.

Barn swallows, he said, were among his best friends. They were insectivores and protected his little garden by eating beetles, ants, grubs, and other pests. And that was how I painlessly learned the word, "insectivores" in spite of my proclivity for tuning out Mr. Irving when he waxed scientific.

He continued, of course, with the information that they were territorial and would chase off any bird that came near his garden to eat the vegetables. Those kinds of birds were called "herbivores." I thought two big words were enough for one day and tried to wind up the lecture by making the inane comment that the swallows' blue coloration was pretty. I mean what could he say about the obvious?

Well, he thought it was interesting I should say that because during the late 1800's the millinary trade valued the barn swallows' brilliant cobalt blue feathers so much that tens of thousands of the birds were netted and killed and might have become extinct but for public outcry, which led to the founding of the first Audubon Society. I decided not to say anything more.

But it wasn't that simple. Mr. Irving never needed anyone else's input to spur him on to greater loquacity. He noted if I watched them closely, I would see that they fed mostly at twilight and at night (who could see them at night, I wondered) and they typically cruised low, inches above the ground or water, snatching bugs out of the air. He went on for a while about migratory patterns and how the *hirundo rustica* differed from other kinds of swallows, but my mind was already elsewhere.

* * *

Twenty years later, I was living in Putney, Vermont, on a lovely country road outside of town. The den in my house faced south and under the eaves of the window snuggled a barn swallows mud nest. For several years running swallows returned to that nest and with their return came memories of Mr. Irving, his yellow boat house, and the "White Ghost."

THE WATERPIPE

The first few warm, sunny days of Spring
would always trigger a restlessness in Grandpa, an
eager anticipation to get to Camp. He found the
frigorific New Hampshire winters a trial to go
through. To him, December through March
presented no winter fairyland of virgin snow
blanketing the earth and coruscating icicles glinting
in pale sunlight. Rather, he saw it as a series of
Job's trials: unremitting cold to be met with hours
spent nursing an old, dirty cantankerous coal
furnace; hours spent shoveling out the walkway, the
driveway, the porch roof, and later reading in the
newspaper of friends and neighbors felled with
heart attacks while engaged in similar endeavors; of
treacherous ice to be carefully walked or driven
upon and to see cars slid off the roads or into each
other, or to hear of Mister so and so who slipped
while walking his dog and broke his hip and left
arm and is still in traction in the hospital; and to
hear of Mrs. Busybody's cellar window broken by a
falling icicle, which let in the freezing night's air,
which froze and burst the main water pipe, which
caused her cellar to flood, which in turn, submerged
her late husband's tool shop and collection of bird
houses that never got hung, and ruined the
Craftsman tools he had acquired over his lifetime
and since his death last year (Yep, heart attack
shoveling out the driveway) she couldn't bring

herself to give away.

Yes, Grandpa hated winter and grudgingly slogged through the dreary, gelid days. But, when those first sun-warmed days heralded that Spring was about to be sprung, he underwent a transformation and became like a racehorse at the gate. His winter torpor vanished and he became practically hyperactive. The man could not sit still. He would wash the car, take off the storm windows, oil and sharpen the lawnmower, and all the while dropping comments, like, "It's going to be ice-out any day now," or "I wonder how the camp survived the winter," or "How will we go about the water pipe this year, Lad?"

The water pipe and ice out were not exactly synonymous, but one couldn't put in the former until the latter had made way, and if Grandpa had his way, we would be wrestling the water pipe into the lake before the last ice floe went out of sight. However, Grandpa liked Grandma's company at Camp, and while Grandma tolerated life at Camp, she detested camping, which meant certain amenities- like running water-- was a prerequisite to her attendance.

Some years ago the Camp's indoor running water system comprised several lengths of iron pipe running from one end, buried a couple of feet below the lake's surface, over the thirty feet of back yard, under the Camp, and ending at a hand pump bolted to a kitchen counter abutting the black, cast iron sink. The system worked and was certainly preferable to hauling buckets of water from the lake. Nevertheless, Grandma, who often did not share Grandpa's utilitarian view of the world, thought a backyard of exposed pipe unsightly and wanted something done about it.

And so it came to pass that on one early May weekend, Grandpa drafted Junior and Uncle Bob for corvée services. Grandma had fried a platter full of eggs, some sunnyside up and the rest easy over. A couple of rashers of bacon, toast with jam, assorted cold cereals, orange juice, and coffee completed the meal. As we all tucked into the vittles, Grandpa said, "Eat up, boys. You're going to need your nourishment today."

Grandma chimed in with her predictable, "I don't want any leftovers to mess with, so Bob, you finish up those eggs. Junior, you haven't had enough bacon. Come on now, boys, eat up." It was seldom worth arguing with her.

After finishing Grandma's cornucopian breakfast, we made our way to the backyard where Grandpa had already laid out spades, a pickax, and a crowbar. Using the water pipe as a guide, he took the crowbar in hand and, with its chiseled edge, drew two parallel lines a foot apart and thirty feet long, running from just inside the double doors that opened to the storage area under the Camp, down to the lake's edge. Turning to us, he said, "That's the outline of the trench we need dug. Make it about a foot-and-a-half deep. The hard part will be the rocks and boulders you run into. Let's hope they're not too big. Take turns, about twenty minutes apiece. Junior, you're the oldest, you get to go first." Junior grumbled and Uncle Bob smiled.

"And what are you going to be doing, Dad, while we do the hard stuff?" queried Junior.

"Just do your job, Son, and don't worry about me. I've got my own job to do." Grandpa turned and walked into the storage area under the Camp. Soon, the muffled sound of wood being sawn attested to his endeavors..

Meanwhile, Junior attacked the outlined trench with a vengeance. He would raise the pick ax with both hands to full stretch overhead and then bring it down as hard as he could, hoping to bury the length of the pick in the ground. Unfortunately, the land around the Camp was mostly rock and stone with only a little dirt so most of his efforts resulted in a dull-sounding "chunk" as the pick penetrated a scant three to four inches before being arrested by a saucer-sized rock. He struck around the area a few more times to free up the offending rock, tossed it to the side, and scooped out what loosened earth there was with the spade, and then repeated the procedure. All too often Junior's pickax blows to the ground emitted a "chink" rather than a "chunk," indicating he had hit another rock just barely covered with dirt and usually resulting in a vibrational shock to his forearms. The "chink" was most often accompanied by a muffled cuss under his breath. Soon a rhythm developed, a kind of tripartite Volga Boatman's chant, which went:

"chink," cuss, scoop..."chink," cuss, scoop....

For Junior, the twenty minute stint couldn't end soon enough, and when it did, he threw the shovel to the ground and said to Uncle Bob, "It's your turn." Without a murmur, Uncle Bob grasped the pick ax and commenced digging.

Junior, still red-faced and sweaty, eyed me and said, "Think you're up for men's work?" Instantly, I knew where this line of questioning was going, but before I could stammer out a reply a *deus ex machina* phenomenon occurred: Grandma opened the kitchen window and hollered out, "How are you boys doing? Are you ready for a coffee break?" While Junior ambled towards the window to respond to Grandma's query, I quickly ducked into the storage area to see what Grandpa was up to.

I heard Junior ask if there were doughnuts to go with the coffee at the same time I asked Grandpa what he was doing. The sounds of wood being sawn had been replaced a few minutes ago by hammering.

"Hello, Lad," Grandpa greeted me . "I see you skeedaddled out of there just in time." Grandpa always amazed me by how much he knew what was going on without saying much about it. Little escaped his pale blue eyes and even less escaped his mouth.

"I'm building what's called a form," he said. He went on to succinctly explain that he was going to install a water tank and an electric pump to bring and store water from the lake to the Camp. When everything was done and working, all one had to do would be to turn a faucet and there would be water, just like at home. We'd have water. No more pump handle to contend with. And best of all, we'd have an indoor toilet. But all of that required that the water tank and electric pump had a solid base upon which to rest. The form he was building would be filled with cement, and when cured, would support the weight of the water-filled tank and pump.

"Where is the toilet going to be?" I asked. He patiently explained that the small storage or 'catch-all' room next to the kitchen door was going to be the new bathroom. We'd find another place to store our coats and stuff.

"But where will the stuff from the toilet go?" Again, Grandpa imperturbably described how the effluent would flush down through a buried inclined pipe to a pit capped with a large, square cement slab located several yards away from the Camp to where the outhouse now stood.

"By next weekend the cement will have cured enough so they can deliver the tank and motor and they'll place them where we need them."

"Why do we have to wait until then?"

"Because the form isn't ready yet; and if they deliver it now, we'd have to manhandle it ourselves when it was ready. And it's heavy."

I thought a minute and said, "But we don't have a pit either and we don't have a trench to bury the pipe in. I'd rather we had the toilet first."

Grandpa nodded. "I know, Lad. But sometimes

you have to take things in order. We can't have a toilet until we have running water first. The toilet is further down the pipeline, literally and figuratively. First things first. It's going to be a long summer and your Dad and uncle need a project to keep them busy. We wouldn't want them bored now, would we. Oh, by the way, this is between you and me. They don't need to know all this yet, understand?" I nodded, feeling important that Grandpa trusted me with this momentous secret and at the same time awed at Grandpa's machinations. Who would have thought that this taciturn gentleman would have created all these plans, step by step and not told anybody - except me.

I turned to go and said, "I won't say a word, Grandpa.

"I know you won't, Lad," he replied, and then added, "And you'll have some work to do on this too, you know." I nodded and walked out of the storage area, being careful to skirt around the corner of the Camp before Junior spied me and commandeered my labors. I wanted some time alone to think about everything Grandpa had confided in me.

I went to the swimming area and picked my way over the littoral until I was out of sight of the Camp. I sat down with my back against the flat side of a sun-warmed granite boulder and stared out at the flat surface of the lake. I briefly considered and stored the information of forms and cement and a solid base for weight-bearing objects and things that shouldn't vibrate. Then I considered at greater length the heady information of planning ahead and of sequence and of priority. Lastly, I considered the business of keeping a secret. I felt important having information that others didn't have, information that they would want to have. If others knew I had it, I would be seen as being important as well. But what would be the consequences if I told? Junior would undoubtedly find a way to avoid the work. Uncle Bob and I would get stuck with more than our share. The project would take much longer. Grandpa would be disappointed in me for giving away his secret and he wouldn't trust me again. That would be unbearable. Then it occurred to me that his telling me could be a test to see if I would keep his secret.

My conversation with Grandpa had exposed me to kinds of thinking to which I was unaccustomed: long-range planning comprising multiple, sequential steps, prioritizing, assessing peoples' strengths and weaknesses, and the consequences of blurting out information just because you have it. As I pondered these issues, my head began to swim. I got to my feet and returned to the Camp - just in time for lunch.

After lunch we returned to the project and I saw that the trench for the water pipe was now about fifteen feet long, almost half way to the water. Junior eyed me predatiously. Holding out the pick ax to me, he said, "Since you goofed off all morning, I think it's your turn and then some."

As I reached for the pick ax, Grandpa gracefully intervened. "You know, Son, the lad doesn't have the muscle yet that you and your brother have, so I think things would go more efficiently if you and Bob switch back and forth with the pick ax and the lad does the shoveling." Junior grumbled something under his breath and held the pick ax out to Uncle Bob. "You go first. I need a few more minutes to digest my lunch."

Grandpa was right. Digging the trench did go faster with Junior and Uncle Bob alternating with the pick and me shoveling. That is until Junior hit a big boulder. It was just under the surface and was substantially larger than the width of the trench and thicker than the trench was deep. This was a major challenge to which Junior did not respond well. He fussed, he cussed, and after the pick ax bounced back off the boulder and grazed his shin, he threw it in a pique and stormed off into the Camp to cage a glass of Grandma's iced tea. At her urging, he took a tray with the pitcher of tea and glasses filled with ice out to the rest of us.

Meanwhile, I had shoveled out the rubble from Junior's efforts while Uncle Bob had loosened up more soil on the other side of the boulder. Grandpa had rummaged around in the storage area under the Camp and returned with three log rollers to use as either wedges or pry blocks in lifting the boulder out of its hole.

Now came the tedious, back-breaking process of ramming the crowbar under the bottom edge of the boulder, placing a pry block of some sort - another rock or log roller just behind the lower end of the crowbar's shaft - and then trying to pry up the boulder a few inches, whereupon someone else would quickly shove a wedge under the boulder. That was the dangerous part for if the crowbar or the boulder slipped while the wedge- placer's hands were under the boulder, a hand could be crushed and hopelessly mangled. Naturally, Junior grabbed the crowbar, leaving Uncle Bob and Grandpa to vie for the dubious honor of wedge-placer. As naturally as Junior had grabbed the crowbar, Grandpa let it be known that he would be the one risking his hands. I would like to say that Grandpa had more faith in Junior than we did, but I suspect the truth is that he was the more self-sacrificing and couldn't bear the thought of Uncle Bob or me losing a hand or two.

Seven courses of wedges and forty-five minutes later, the boulder - a good three feet across and at least a foot-and-a-half thick and weighing several hundred pounds - was levered out of the hole. All hands and feet unscathed. The crater it left behind was about five feet in diameter and two-and-a-half deep. It made our twenty-five foot trench look puny in comparison, like a long, slender river debouching into a large lake.

Uncle Bob was about to begin prying up the boulder to tip it end for end towards the lake's edge when Grandpa stopped him. "Getting the waterpipe in is the priority here, Son. The clean-up can be done later." Again, I was reminded of the lesson:

never forget priorities, first things first, the least important goes last.

Soon after, the remaining five feet of trench was dug and the pipe laid in the bottom. The task at the water end of the pipe was the next major challenge: to lower the end of the pipe into the water to rest about a foot off the bottom and six feet down. Because ice out had occurred only a couple of weeks past and the water temperature was just a few degrees above freezing, no one wanted to go into the water. Grandpa noted that in the past they had used the rowboat as a makeshift floating platform from which two people (one to steady the boat in the water with the oars and the other to lower the free end of the waterpipe by means of a long length of clothesline looped under the pipe's end). Grandpa would be on shore giving direction and joining the pipe ends together with a threaded sleeve or coupling.

It didn't take long to wrestle the rowboat out from the storage area under the Camp and push-pull it on log rollers to the water's edge. My job: grab a pine log after the rowboat had rolled over it and lug it as fast as I could to a few feet in front of the lumbering boat and place the log in the correct alignment so the boat remained on course. I had visions of being a Hebrew slave in Pharaonic Egypt with a half-built pyramid shimmering in the blistering heat of the Valley of Kings. Simon Lagree cracked his whip and shouted at me and I suddenly realized two things: first, I had mixed my metaphors, and second, Junior was yelling at me to stop day dreaming and hustle the log; he didn't have all day.

Junior pre-empted the position of oarsman, leaving Uncle Bob the more delicate task of holding the waterpipe in a straight line from shore and lowering it down through the water to rest on a submerged cinder block. This required him to kneel or stand on the rowboat's stern seat so he could peer down into the water, spot the cinder block, and carefully lower the pipe with the looped clothesline to rest it on the block. If he missed, the block and the pipe landed on the silty lake bottom, the metal filter on the tip would sink into the silt and become plugged. Then he would have to haul the pipe out of the water, clean it and the pipe out, and start all over. No wonder Junior had snagged the oarsman position.

It was a warm late spring day. After a long winter with more than the usual amounts of snow, the snow and ice melt had filled the lake to overflowing. Some surrounding low-lying areas were flooded. A few zealous fishermen were on the lake, the distant bee-buzz of their outboard motors signaling their move from one favored spot to another. There was not the slightest wafture of a breeze; the lake's surface was still as the proverbial mirror, except for the occasional series of waves from a distant fisherman's boat, which rocked the rowboat long after the warning bee-buzz faded into stillness. It was tacitly understood that it was part of

Junior's job to warn Uncle Bob of the approaching waves before they rocked the boat so he wouldn't be caught unaware in his carefully balanced kneeling and fall overboard.

Uncle Bob grumbled that he couldn't see the lake bottom unless he leaned over far enough for his shadow to dispel the surface reflection and leaning that far jeopardized his range of stability. Junior commented that they could put me in the boat to hold him by the seat of his pants so he wouldn't fall over. There must have been something in the tone of Junior's voice that prompted Uncle Bob to reject the offer.

As Uncle Bob leaned, teetered, lowered and raised the pipe, Junior baited him about not being able to do a simple thing as dropping a pipe on a block. Uncle Bob countered, saying the reflection threw him off. I recalled Mr. Irving once explaining refraction to me when I asked him why my homemade fish spear always appeared bent when I put it in the water. He said something about how a light wave changes direction when it passes from one medium to another of different density. Since the lake was calm at the time I didn't know what waves had to do with anything, never mind a light wave.

I looked up when I heard Grandpa tell Junior to straighten out and come to the left more, the pipe was straying off line. Junior muttered something in response but the sudden high pitched whine of a motorboat drowned out his words. The motorboat came zooming full bore around the point and only fifty feet from shore. Grandpa waved his arms to get Junior's attention. Uncle Bob, teetering in a precarious half-crouch position on the rowboat's stern seat and holding the water pipe by the clothesline sling, lifted his gaze from the lakebed's bottom to Grandpa's waving arms. The waves from the motorboat came rushing toward the rowboat. I waved my arms at Uncle Bob and pointed to the fast approaching waves, thinking of course he would understand what my wildly gesticulating arms meant to convey. The first wave hit, the rowboat scended, and Junior, untrammeled by any bonds of fraternal loyalty or concern, seized his opportunity and dug the oars deeply in the water and heaved as hard as he could. The rowboat lunged forward and upward, just as the natural gurgitation of the wave rolled under it. Quick as a wink, Uncle Bob plunged face first into the freezing water. The splash wasn't nearly as impressive as it might have been.

Then, several things occurred simultaneously: Junior burst into uncontrollable laughter, Uncle Bob broke surface yelling in indignant outrage and began splashing his way to shore. Grandpa put two fingers in his mouth and gave a shrill whistle to get Junior's attention, accompanied by a stiff come here motion with his arm…and the motorboat raced off in the distance.

Everything that followed was anticlimactic. Grandpa helped Uncle Bob ashore over the seawall and told him to go inside and get into dry clothes.

He told Junior to get out of the boat right now and I should row the boat back to its mooring in the cove and go in the Camp.

I don't know what Grandpa said to Junior, but I expect it was a dressing down, brief and to the point. I do know when Junior came into the Camp a short while later, he was subdued and kept to himself. Grandpa talked with Grandma on the porch and all I heard of that conversation was a spluttered," Well, I never!"

Over the next several weekends and under Grandpa's watchful eye, Junior completed the project by himself. Oh yeah, one more thing, when Uncle Bob fell in the lake he dropped the water pipe dead center on the cinder block.

THE ICE-HOUSE

Weekend trips to Camp evolved into a predictable sequence of activities. Grandpa arrived home from his second-shift job at 11:30 p.m. Grandma was packed and waiting. I'd have gone resisting to bed hours before and be sleeping soundly. Grandpa'd load up the car with their old blue suitcase and various cardboard boxes, some of which contained the tools for whatever repair job at Camp he had chosen to do that weekend. He'd return from the car to fetch me out of bed. Sometimes I'd wake up and walk to the car under my own power, but usually he carried me like a sack of potatoes and deposited me on the back seat, which was my designated spot whenever the three of us traveled. If it was just Grandpa and me in the car, I'd ride shotgun and feel rather grownup. We then embarked in the middle of the night on the hour-long drive to camp.

About three miles from Camp we'd approach the town of Bristol by coming down the long steep hill by the fire station and enter the town square. A square patch of grass with an antique cannon and neatly stacked pyramid of cannon balls heralded the town green.

It was always a family puzzle why I invariably woke up as we descended this hill. Whether it was a sort of spiritual connection being re-established or rather a manifestation of some natural law, like when one brings the opposite poles of two magnets closer and closer until they finally sense each other and then suddenly--click-- they fly together. I could believe either speculation. Certainly some principle of attraction was at work.

"Good, we're almost there," I'd drowsily announce and then promptly fall asleep again. Sometimes I'd stay awake long enough to hear Grandpa's chuckle and Grandma's louder, unrestrained laughter and usual comment, "That's our little navigator."

Upon our arrival at Camp, I'd sometimes wake up again and stagger up the narrow staircase to my bedroom. Other times Grandpa'd carry me. Years later, I would carry my own two sons up that same narrow staircase.

Saturday morning we rose at the usual weekday time so we could have breakfast and ride to town to do our shopping before the out-of-towners descended on the First National store to do theirs. Somehow I never thought of ourselves as out-of-towners. I just assumed that four generations of family at the Camp gave us "local" status.

On our return trip to Camp, we swung onto the West Shore Road for a short distance to the Ice-House to pick up our block of ice for our refrigeration needs for the weekend. I looked forward to that part of the ride because the place fascinated me. I'd sit impatiently in the car's back seat, mentally willing us to get there faster.

The dark bulk of the Ice-House loomed

between the winding road and the lake. Towering among the maple trees, its two-and-a-half story wooden bulk exuded an ambience of solidity, of permanence, as though it had occupied that particular spot beside the lake for ages. The massive barn door slid open along its front by iron wheels bolted to the top of the door which rolled along a steel rail affixed just above the lintel. The door could be slid open from a few inches to a span of ten feet. Its dark, mysterious interior was dimly lit by a single light bulb hanging from a cord from the ceiling. The aromatic smell of wood resin from sawdust permeated the air. Inside, it was cool and damp. The sound of water dripping was ever present. Hundreds upon hundreds of blocks of ice were stacked atop each other, much like bales of hay in a hayloft. Each block was generously packed on all sides by a thick layer of sawdust.

Mr. Irving later explained to me that the purpose of the sawdust was not just insulation, as I had conjectured, but it also performed another very important function of preventing all those blocks of ice from fusing together into a solid mass. He said something about ice under pressure liquefying on the stressed surfaces and then fusing together, similar to two pieces of steel welded together. The sawdust prevented the surfaces from touching, so they couldn't join.

Grandpa parked the car close to the entrance and went to talk to the ice men. The ice men always impressed me. They wore brown leather aprons, a leather belt, and a cape over one shoulder. They had wide shoulders, bulging biceps, and corded forearms - a little boy's inspiration. They reminded me of the Charles Atlas ads I had seen in the back of certain magazines.

On the inside wall over the cash box, several photographs were tacked up. They showed different phases of ice harvesting. The first photo was of an ice man holding a huge, six foot saw with giant triangular teeth with which they cut the ice. The next showed the frozen lake proximate to the ice house. There were large, square holes cut in the ice that resembled swimming pools. Another showed a team of four work horses pulling a sledge loaded with blocks of ice. That photo reminded me of the oxen-pulling contests at the state fair. The load of ice looked impossibly heavy. The last one was a group shot of several ice men in their leathers. Some were smiling into the camera and others just looked tired.

One of the ice men, having taken Grandpa's order, disappeared into the twilight of the icehouse's interior. He emerged with a block of ice impaled between the barbed pincers of ice tongs and slung over his shoulder. I don't know how much a block of ice weighed, but I knew I couldn't lift it off the ground. I know this because on one occasion I brashly asked if I could try. At a nearly imperceptible nod from my Grandpa, the ice man laughingly set a block on the floor and motioned me forward to give it a try. I bent over slightly, grasped

the wooden handles of the ice tongs and heaved
with all my might. It barely slid an inch to the left.
There was no vertical movement. Dismayed, but not
willing to admit defeat, I huffed and puffed, jerked
and heaved. It scarcely lurched back the scant inch
to its original position. The ice men and Grandpa
were chuckling and exchanging encouraging
comments, which I barely heard. I finally ceased
embarrassing myself, saying I'd be back next
summer to lift it. Somehow, I forgot about that self-
imposed challenge in the subsequent years and my
Grandpa had the good grace never to remind me.

The ice man wedged the ice block between the
steel back bumper and trunk of the car and Grandpa
slowly drove the remaining mile-and-a-half to
Camp. He always made the same comment, "You
know, Lad, it's only an eighth of a mile to the Camp
across the water. You can see it from here. If the
lake was frozen, we could drive straight over and be
there by now."

*　*　*

As he spoke these words, little did Grandpa
know that less than a decade earlier Junior had done
exactly that - sort of. He was engaged to my mother,
about to be married, and eagerly looking for the
opportunity to have some quality "alone time" with
her. Winter had arrived early and the lake was
frozen over. The Ice-House was already harvesting
its blocks from the lake, great gaping holes in the

surface testified to the yield. The dirt road into Camp was blanketed with several inches of snow. No one would be driving in -- a perfect location for a tryst. Junior correctly reasoned that if they were harvesting ice than the ice was thick enough to drive a vehicle on.

He borrowed Grandpa's car and he and my mother drove to the foot of the lake, onto the lake, and across the lake to Camp, where they spent the afternoon enjoying "alone time." The Glenwood provided heat when their own flagged.

The sun sets early in winter and before they knew it, darkness had descended. There was no moon and they had to drive back across the ice, avoiding the open trenches of recently removed ice. The freezing temperatures had caused a thin skin of ice to form over the holes and in the headlights the entire lake's surface appeared the same gray color. One couldn't see the darkness of the deep water under the thin ice until one was right on top of it. As my mother related this story to me years later, I had visions of African pit traps, dug deeply enough for their yawning maws to swallow elephants. Apparently Junior had similar thoughts because he had my mother keep her car door open - as he did his own - just in case they accidentally drove into one of these holes, they might have a chance to escape. She remembered him calling them the *car*nivorous holes and laughing uproariously at his own joke. She was less amused. The return trip over the lake was harrowing, but without incident.

* * *

The tricky and even slower pace of this return
trip to Camp occurred when we turned off the
secondary paved road and onto the dirt track. That
track was narrow, with space for only one car at a
time, and few places along its half-mile length to
pull over to let someone coming the other way to
pass. It was up and down, serpentine, bumpy, and
rutted. Grandpa drove at a snail's pace to insure the
ice block didn't jar loose and fall off.

Personally, I thought Grandpa overdid his slow,
cautious approach. Perhaps it was a part of his being
so old and conservative, until one day we rounded a
corner and came unexpectedly face-to-face with a
car coming towards us. In his surprise, Grandpa
jammed on the brakes. All of us rocked forward,
then back, and a soft thud was heard from the rear
of the car. Grandpa cursed, Grandma said, "Oh,
dear," and the car in front of us blared its horn.

Grandpa got out of the car and, ignoring the
opposing vehicle, walked to the rear where
Grandma and I distinctly heard him curse again.
Like an echo, Grandma repeated her previous, "Oh,
dear," this time more emphatically. As though not
to be outdone, the other vehicle impatiently honked
its horn again.

I scurried out of my back seat and around to the
back of the car to see what was going on. In the
middle of the right side, tire-rutted road lay the ice
block - in pieces. Dirt, dust, a few pine needles and

leaves, covered them. The sudden car stop had rocked the block off the bumper, where it fell upon the high point of a mostly-buried rock, shattering it. The shards of ice glistened in the sunlight like scattered diamonds. Only two or three chunks were worth saving. As we stared at this mini disaster, the silence was penetrated by the strident honk of the other vehicle's horn.

Grandpa opened the car's trunk, picked up the largest chunks of ice, fitted them between their blue suitcase and cardboard boxes, and said quietly, "Get in the car, Lad. We can't do anymore here." We got into the car and he slowly backed up to where he could pull off and let the other vehicle go by. As it passed, the occupants shouted something to us, and we could tell by their faces they were frustrated by having to wait for us, but with our windows closed we couldn't make out exactly what they said. Grandpa never looked at them or said a word. They had out-of-state license plates. Grandma spluttered, "Wouldn't you just know it. Out-of-staters!"

When we arrived at Camp, we took the groceries inside. Grandpa put the few chunks of ice in the ice chest and announced he was returning to the Ice-House for another block and I was to help Grandma. Apparently he needed time alone. Grandma instructed me to put the perishables away. That meant in the ice chest, in which there was little ice.

The ice chest was a beauty: golden oak with brass latches. It looked more like a piece of fine furniture than an appliance. The top half contained the block of ice; the bottom half held the perishables. Below the ice was a tray, tin I think, that collected the melted ice water and kept the food below dry. Other models had a drainage valve and a rubber hose that exited the back or side of the chest. I remember Grandma constantly admonishing me to "not just stand there with the door open." That admonition carried over to the electric refrigerator at home as well.

By the principle of heat transfer, the cold air from the ice drifted down to cool the perishables in the lower compartment and the warmer air drifted up to gradually melt the ice so a circular kind of air movement occurred…or something like that. Mr. Irving explained it all to me once, but all I really remember thinking about was that we had an electric refrigerator at home, and the Camp had been wired for electricity just a few years before, so why didn't the grand folks simply buy a refrigerator and stop all this ice-lugging business? Mr. Irving once commented that the Chinese had harvested and stored ice for cooling purposes a thousand years before the birth of Christ and we hadn't progressed much beyond that. I couldn't remember how Mr. Irving kept his own perishables cold, or even if he had perishables, beyond what he grew in his raised beds.

I think it was the following year that the Camp acquired its first electric refrigerator. It lasted a very long time.

THE ROWBOAT

"Believe me, my young friend, there is nothing
- absolutely nothing - half so much worth doing as
simply messing about in boats."

   —Ratty, <u>Wind in the Willows</u>

When World War II broke out and America
joined the fray, a wave of patriotism swept over this
country similar to that evidenced in World War I.
Flags fluttered, banners and bunting were proudly
displayed, victory gardens planted, war bonds
bought, and parades honored those in service.
Servicemen were respected and emulated by little
boys. Uncle Bob enlisted in the U.S. Navy - and
Junior became a conscientious objector.

Why Junior was so contrary by nature is
anybody's guess, and I'm sure my grandparents
must have pondered that question innumerable
times. While he wanted to make some kind of
statement by refusing to carry a gun, he didn't want
to miss out on any accolades either - not to mention
avoiding my grandparent's displeasure - so he
joined the Merchant Marines and became a radio
operator. My mother once said he looked very
dashing in his uniform.

After war's end he returned from the Merchant
Marines with an appreciation for boats which soon
coalesced into a decision to repair and restore
Grandpa's five-year-old rowboat. Yes, the boat

which replaced the one Junior had run aground a few year's previously. True to his fashion, he needed a helper and he volunteered me.

As I recall, we began the boat project early in the season. I think the same spring day that we put in the water pipe at Camp and hooked it up to the pump we also dragged the rowboat out from its winter storage place under the Camp and placed it upside down on two pine roller logs.

Junior told me to dust off the winter's accumulation of dust, leaves, and mouse droppings, and then flip the boat over and brush out the inside as well. Having turned the boat upside down once more, the real work commenced.

Junior gave me two putty knives: one with a three-inch blade, the other with a one-inch blade. He demonstrated how he wanted all the loose paint (of which there was remarkably little) scraped off and then, more difficult, how to scrape the paint that wasn't loose but could be persuaded to lose its grip. However, I was not to gouge the wood-- ever. The fun and novelty wore off in about ten minutes.

Junior explained that I should work from the top down so the chips and debris didn't impede the area being scraped. I soon learned to rely on the putty knives and not my fingernails to prize up a paint chip after a particularly tenacious chip jammed into the quick under my fingernail.

It took me a whole weekend to scrape that boat inside and out, floorboards and seats. But I was looking forward to painting; that would be fun.

Now Junior appeared and informed me there were a couple of things to do before painting. The next step was sandpapering the edges where paint had been scraped off and there was a tiny ridge between the remaining paint and the bare wood. It seemed unnecessarily picky but Junior said there was a right way to do things and a wrong way, and someday I would appreciate knowing the right way.

I learned about sanding. I learned about curving sandpaper around fingers and pencils and wooden blocks. I learned about friction burns and blisters. I learned sanding takes about as long as scraping and is every bit as much fun. I also learned that a Junior project didn't entail much of Junior's labor.

At one point during the scraping and the sanding, Mr. Irving appeared. He had brought some fresh blackberries that he picked that morning for my grandparents. He stopped, puffed on his pipe, and strolled around the overturned rowboat, looking thoughtful. He finally asked if I was up on my Greek mythology. When I shook my head, he puffed more fiercely on his pipe, sending blue clouds of Prince Albert into the air, harrumphed, and said I should get hold of Bullfinch and check out the Augean Stables and Sisyphus as well - I might appreciate the similarities. He strolled away to find Grandpa, leaving me to wonder what bullfinches had to do with anything.

The next step, Junior explained, was fundamental in making the boat watertight. He pulled a dark, brown ropy thing out of a box. It smelled wonderful: sharp and resinous. He called it oakum. He demonstrated pressing the tarry, fibrous oakum strands into a barely visible seam between the ship-lapped boards of the rowboat's port side. He packed the seam tight by pressing the oakum, strand by strand, with a putty knife. The oakum fibers were treated with a tar-like substance that was waterproofing. It took me about half a day to fill every crack and seam with oakum. It required kerosene to clean my hands when I finished. I remember Grandpa shaking his head as he poured it into a coffee can for me to clean up

"Is it ready to paint yet?" I asked Junior.

"No, But you're getting closer."

The next step was caulking, which entailed squeezing white caulk out of a tube over the oakum-filled cracks and seams and pressing it in with the flat of a putty knife and smoothing it out so it was flush with the surface. This went faster than the oakum business.

"It's got to be ready for painting now."

"Not quite. Almost."

"What do you mean, almost?" I asked suspiciously.

"Linseed oil."

What's that?" I queried.

"It's like painting, only it's not. You'll like it."

"Huh?"

Linseed oil, I learned, was made from pressed flaxseeds and used in paints and resins, and in this instance was a wonderful waterproofing substance when applied to bare wood surfaces. It sounded to me like Junior had been talking with Mr. Irving lately.

Junior was right. Applying the linseed oil with a brush was a lot like painting, except its pale yellow translucency wasn't nearly as satisfying. Paint leaves a visible record of accomplishment. There's no doubt about what you have done with paint.

"You're really close now," Junior said placatingly.

"Yeah?

"Just a couple more details."

"I knew it."

The couple of details were primer coats - two of them - over the linseed coats, which covered the bare wood. The primer coats looked just like white paint to me and prompted my question of why not just use the white paint since the boat was to be painted white anyway? The impatient answer was predictable: because there is the right way to do things and a wrong way....

Finally, after many days, I painted the rowboat. The inside was painted first because Junior didn't want the freshly painted bottom to sit on the log rollers. I stopped myself from asking what difference it made which side was painted first because the answer suddenly hit me. And that thought led to several others related to the sequence of things and how some steps had to occur before other steps or a process just wouldn't be right.

Something would be lacking or a vulnerability created or in some major or minor way the whole just wouldn't be a complete whole…. Just maybe there was something to this right way and wrong way to do things after all.

I explained my epiphany to Mr. Irving later - I didn't want to talk to Junior; he'd take too much pleasure in saying, "I told you so." Mr. Irving nodded sagely and replied that was the nature of propaedeutics: often one had to have an introductory experience before a full understanding of them occurred, the former serving as an preface to the latter. I briefly wondered why most things were never simple with him.

When I was at home, I rode my bike everywhere. When I was not in school or sleeping I was pedaling somewhere. Often there was no destination in mind, I just rode for sheer pleasure. The rowboat became my Camp-equivalent to my bike at home. While I was at Camp I was in the rowboat most of my waking hours. I rowed forwards. I rowed backwards. I sculled with one oar. I paddled it with one oar as an ungainly canoe. The rowboat became like an appendage. I'm surprised I didn't try to sleep in it.

I raced from one end of the cove to the other as fast as I could go and then back. I grew calluses on my hands. My shoulders and forearms got bigger. One day, in the heat of some imaginary race, I was huffing and puffing and straining to go faster and create a more impressive wake behind the boat, the roar of the imagined crowd loud in my ears, the screws to the left oarlock ripped out of the wood, the oar went flying in air rather than water, and I went flying backwards. I landed in a sprawl in the bottom of the boat, hitting my head on the bow seat on the way down. Everything got dark and sparkly for a while.

I and my chariot of dampened fire limped back to Camp. (I know I'm mixing metaphors and neither chariots nor rowboats limp, but that's how it felt.) The imagined crowd had lost interest and disappeared and instead there stood Grandpa. He was not impressed. Grandma tut tutted about the growing lump on the back of my head and put ice in a washcloth on it. Her fussing about me was gratifying, especially in light of Grandpa's lack of approbation. That night as I lay in my bed, I had a complexity of emotions and thoughts jumbling about in my head: there was the adolescent pride that I had been strong enough to rip the oarlock screws out of the boat's gunwale; there was the warrior's badge of honor - the bump on the head - testifying to my efforts; there was the impatience of waiting the couple of days for the oarlock to be repaired and I wouldn't be rowing anywhere; and then there was Grandpa's displeasure at the damage done; and all that was the result of something that wasn't even real. There was no race, no crowd, no cheers, just a fiction, a young boy's imagination.

* * *

Not surprisingly, it wasn't long before the cove had been thoroughly examined and I wanted new territory to explore. Also, not surprisingly, Grandpa had been anticipating that. I had begun my cleverly designed dialectic to support taking the rowboat out on the main body of the lake when he held up his hand stopping me. He said the main lake was substantially larger and could be a whole lot rougher than the cove. I knew that. In fact, that was the major part of its allure for me, but I wasn't going to tell him that. He nodded his head toward the island opposite the Camp. Its distance from the Camp was perhaps three times the width of the cove's opening. Grandpa continued, as soon as I could swim to the island and back I could take the rowboat out in the main body of the lake. Somehow I wasn't surprised. Endurance swim training began that afternoon.

By the end of summer I was rowing all over the lake, discovering other coves, beaches, islands, and feeder rivers. I loved it. But my favorite excursions were when the north wind whistled down the lake, raising the whitecaps to heights that drove the summer boaters inside their cottages and I had the lake to myself. My Grandma fussed and told me to be sensible and stay inside. Grandpa would reassuringly pat her arm and tell her the lad would be careful and then give me a piercing look that said I darn well better.

The thrill of rowing up a white-capped wave, all surging motion and hissing gurgling noise, feeling the boat power out of the crest and then crash down into the following trough, spray flying out, was like a drug. I couldn't get enough of it. Sometimes I caught a glimpse of Grandpa watching me from the patio and I pretended not to notice.

Less than a quarter mile up the lake there was a channel that ran between the island and a reef. This reef was much larger than the one in the cove and consisted of twenty or more house-sized boulders that just barely broke the surface of the lake, except in the fall when the lake level was drawn down. I would head for this reef and play among the boulders, spinning on the top of a wave, turning to avoid one boulder, back paddling to avoid another. Occasionally the rowboat crunched into a rock less visible than the others or grazed still another because I misjudged distance and the force of the wave - and each time I imagined Grandpa's patient but disapproving stare. I knew by late fall I'd have a lot of sanding and repainting to do.

Years later, the rowboat gave way to a sailboat and then to kayaks, but the same love of playing in the waves continued unabated.... And did I mention that Junior used the rowboat exactly twice that season?

BLOODSUCKERS, BEACH SAND, AND BLUEBERRIES

When my great grandfather built the Camp as his fishing shack, I presume it also represented to him that place to which he escaped from whatever he did most of the time that was not nearly as pleasurable. That was certainly my grandpa's reason for driving an hour from home every weekend from ice-out in Spring to the second hard frost in Fall. The Camp was his sanctuary, his refuge from the regular work-a-day world he found little pleasure in. His ultimate pleasure was simply sitting in a chair by the lakeside watching the shifting colors on distant Mount Cardigan and Mount Tenney as the occasional cloud passed over and the play of errant breezes rippled the lake surface. For my father, myself, and years later, my two sons, the Camp was a place to play in the sun and water, and like our progenitors, a place to get away from our regular lives.

The lake was the focus of most of our play. We had other forms of recreation available: horseshoes, badminton, reading, cards, and various board games, such as Monopoly, checkers, chess, Flinch, and so on, but it was always to the water that we were primarily drawn, like salmon to the sea. Boating, swimming, horsing around in the water, or just sitting in a tire tube and cooling off. There were only two problems: bloodsuckers and rocks.

For a few years the swimming area was

infested by leeches. We called them bloodsuckers. I remember Mr. Irving once telling me there were several species of leeches, terrestrial and aquatic, and some in the latter category had been used in days gone by in medicine for bloodletting and removing infected tissue. I wondered at the time if he spoke from personal experience.

Our bloodsuckers were gray-green in color and ranged in size from three-quarters if an inch to three inches in length. If they stuck to you long enough their underbellies changed to a reddish-brown. When you pulled one off, your skin would appear pinkish-brown and leaving an angry suck mark. I was surprised that you couldn't feel them on you and because of that, we checked each other periodically for the little suckers (pun intended). Mr. Irving explained that the reason we couldn't feel them was that they secreted a substance that had anesthetic properties, which enabled them to feed on blood without the host's awareness. He claimed they had further value in that their buccal glands exuded a grayish-white material called hirudin, which was used in medicine chiefly as an anticoagulant. While all that was interesting, I had a more primitive focus of attention. When we found them, we had a special boulder that we put them on and then we smashed them with a rock. It reminded me of an Aztec blood sacrifice. After a few years the bloodsuckers disappeared. Given their profusion, I can't imagine we killed them all. I still wonder what happened to them, why they left and where they went.

The second problem was rocks. To get to the water one had to clamber over the rock-strewn shoreline to the water's edge, where the rocks continued, only covered by increasing depths of water. The rocks hurt the feet and they were slippery. To slip on the rocks and then fall upon them was painful and potentially dangerous. Thus evolved the tradition of each generation clearing out and enlarging the previous generation's swimming area.

What lay under the littoral was a composite of small rocks, gravel, silt, and occasional patches of sand. Sometimes in those patches of sand, I would find small swirls of reddish-purple, where ever-so-fine crystals of garnet had leached out of a nearby rock to form a nascent Mandala. To my young mind those intertwined strands of garnet in the sand were arcane runes laid down by magical forces at work.

As the years passed, the Camp's swimming area gradually expanded and the footing became more tolerable. Nevertheless, it was a common practice for most of us to wear sandals, old sneakers, or rubber bathing slippers.

The rock-clearing effort was aided and abetted by the local township at the southern end of the lake, which in late fall drew down a few feet of water so to reduce the amount of spring flooding, and more to our purpose, so waterfront landowners could do necessary repairs to seawalls, docks, boathouses, and shorelines. For us, it meant we could rake up the small rocks and stones in the swimming area and use them as fill in the cracks in the sea-walled, horseshoe-shaped swimming area. Standing on dry land with rake in hand on what a few weeks past was below several feet of water was an alien experience, like being on the moon's surface. I guess if I had lived on the coast and was familiar with the tides coming in and going out it wouldn't have seemed strange at all. Nonetheless, the feeling of an alien landscape was further enhanced by the fact that the lake was now practically devoid of boats, water skiers, fishermen and the similar hustle and bustle that characterized a typical summer's afternoon on the lake. The summer crowd had left, gone back to whence they came, to take up the reins of their everyday lives. The few isolated hold-outs were busily engaged in their own last minute repairs before they, too, returned to distant homes.

Grandpa and I raked up the small rocks in the swimming area, scooped them into pails that I carried to the seawall and dumped them into the cracks and joints of the large, flat stones capping the wall. Sometimes what appeared to be a partially buried small rock would turn out to be a much larger rock whose top had just become exposed, similar to an iceberg, whose vast bulk remained submerged below the surface. These we dug up, pried out, and rolled away. Of course that left the problem of a small crater-sized hole to deal with. On one such occasion Grandpa said to me, "You know, Lad, it's never going to be like a beach." And that started my mind a-whirling.

A quarter mile or so across the water was a sizable island. It hosted one of the many summer camps around for children and young teenagers. The north shore of this island was almost entirely sandy beach with only an occasional granite erratic poking its head above water, like an inquisitive seal. The boys and their counselors had left for the season, leaving the wooden board and batten housing units - boasting such brave names as Sioux, Cheyenne, and Comanche carved on wooden plaques over the doorways - standing desolate as a ghost town. And all that sand….

That evening, about a half-hour before sundown, I loaded the rowboat with all the pails and buckets I could find, and a shovel we had used for road repair. I shoved off and began rowing, heading for the northern tip of the island. There wasn't a breath of breeze and the lake's surface was motionless. In fact, the whole lake was quiet that late fall evening and I imagined the sound of the oarlocks carried across the water and into every camp for miles around. If it did, there were very few to hear it and those few that did likely surmised it signaled a fisherman rowing home.

As I bent my back to the oars, the rowboat skimmed lightly over the glass-smooth surface. I tried to remember what Mr. Irving had tried to explain to me not so long ago about the sun causing the generation of warm air masses, which in turn generated air currents and breezes and sunset causing the opposite effect and that was why he chose evening for his cruises in the White Ghost. I didn't pay much attention at the time, but as I pulled on the oars and the boat surged across the quiet water, Mr. Irving's explanation came to mind. It occurred to me then, briefly, that maybe I should pay closer attention to his ramblings in the future.

It didn't take long to arrive at my destination. The last thirty feet I rowed hard to drive the bow of the boat up onto the beach just beyond the water's edge so I could hop out without getting wet. Armed with pails and shovel, I walked about ten feet and started digging, filling the pails with fine, golden beach sand. The hole was two feet deep when I realized I couldn't just leave a gaping hole in the middle of the beach. Not only could someone step into it and break a leg, but it looked terrible, like a miniature strip mine. In addition, it would be obvious that someone had been digging up sand, and not just to build sand castles.

I dumped the buckets back into the hole, refilling it, and then started skimming the top two to three inches of sand from the beach with the edge of the shovel. The sand removal was not nearly so obvious. It didn't take long to fill the pails a second time. I lugged them two by two to the rowboat and placed them in the bow and behind the rower's seat located midship (if that term can be used for a rowboat).

Ready to row back to Camp, I grasped the

rowboat's prow and heaved - and almost fell to my knees. The bow, laden with the sand's weight, hadn't budged an inch. I was going to get wet after all. After lightening the load by removing the buckets of sand from the bow, I was able to launch the rowboat. I removed my sneakers and socks, rolled up my pant legs, and carried the pails one by one with both hands to the boat bobbing gently up and down a couple feet off shore.

I remember the feel of the sand under my naked feet, firm but smooth, formfitting, still warm from the heat of the day. There was nothing hard or jagged to abuse the feet. This was how I imagined our little swimming area at Camp to be. As I rowed in the deepening twilight a memory flashed into my mind of a late summer's afternoon at Camp a few years before. I was playing near the horseshoe pit in back of Camp. I heard the sound of oarlocks coming from the cove, next to our blueberry bushes. A young couple and two little girls were talking and laughing and stripping off the blueberries overhanging the water, filling up a dented metal boat bailer and red plastic party cups.

Outraged at this flagrant transgression, I stomped onto plain view and yelled in my best eight-year-old indignation, "Hey, this is private property. Leave our blueberries alone."

"Whoa there, Sonny," replied the man. "The lake is public property. Nobody owns it."

"Yeah, well the blueberries are on our land and we own that, so we own the blueberries, so go away."

I saw the man and woman look behind me. Then she looked at him and nodded her head towards the cove's entrance, indicating they should leave in that direction - now. I looked behind me and saw Grandpa, alerted by the commotion, striding towards us.

"Okay, Sonny," said the man, "We're leaving." He began rowing away.

"Stingy!" shouted one of the little girls. I was struck by the resentful look she gave me.

I turned to my grandfather, who had just arrived at my side. "They were stealing our blueberries," I said, and in that statement I expected him to understand the situation, share in my indignation, and validate my perception of robbery - a tall order for a five-word sentence.

He watched them for a moment rowing away, then said, "Maybe they didn't understand it as stealing. You can't see the Camp all that well from the water because of all the trees and bushes."

I was speechless and dumfounded. How could he not see the obvious?

I pondered this memory as I rowed. I noticed that the weight of the beach sand made the rowboat much harder to row. It was heavy, slow, low in the water, and sluggish to turn. With each stroke of the oars the burden seemed to increase.

It was almost dark when I rowed into the Camp's swimming area. I offloaded the pails of beach sand, which somehow seemed heavier than ever. As I made my way into Camp, I was still musing over stolen blueberries and the beach sand sitting in pails. I don't remember reaching any conclusion to my musings, but I do remember that the next day, after I thoughtfully poured out the beach sand in the swimming area - it turned out to be a pitifully small amount when spread out - I never went after beach sand again.

THE PATIO

The lake's shoreline, with the exception of a few sandy beaches, was rockbound. Our Camp's perimeter was no exception. By dint of brute physical labor and crowbar, each generation within the family had taken it as a personal challenge to enlarge upon the previous generation's efforts to create a rock-free swimming area. Rocks cleared from it were carefully fitted into a small, semi-circular sea wall, which bounded our tiny beach. Each generation took it upon itself to tear down a section of the existing sea wall, clear a few more feet, and rebuild the sea wall farther back. Each time the bathing area was enlarged by a possible yard.

By the time I was old enough to participate in the intergenerational rock-piling challenge, the swimming area had spread to a thirty-five-foot radius—big enough in my mind. So I decided to build a patio on the top side of part of the sea wall.

My mental blueprint of the patio increased its height by two feet, just above the spring high water mark. Measuring about fifteen feet in length by eight feet in width, it would be capped in a couple inches of poured and leveled cement to prevent chairs from wobbling and tipping.

It soon became evident that to build up the patio to my proposed two foot height would require much more stone than I originally thought. To fulfill that requirement meant clearing more bathing area after all. Nuts!

Now, as I figured it, my time and effort expenditure had just doubled. In actuality, what was originally to be a two-week summer vacation plus a few weekends' project became two summers' vacations plus most weekends of the next two springs, summers, and falls - two years. Nuts.

Around the lake there were many sea walls, some stone docks, and some patios. The older ones were of laid-up stone, which required repair every year. I was reminded of Robert Frost's line;

"Something there is that doesn't like a wall,
That wants it down."

True for all laid stone, I thought, whether it's sea walls, docks, or foundations (the Camp had a laid stone foundation).

Other laid-stone sea walls had cement caps, which had to be repaired less often. Still others had cement both on top and face. These lasted the longest. But even they succumbed eventually to the ravages of ice and pounding waves. My idea was not only to cement both the face and top but each internal course of stone as well, thus creating a solid block of stone and cement that offered no cracks or crevices for water to infiltrate, freeze, expand and do its damage. Having no experience with this sort of thing, little did I realize just how much cement this would require.

I ordered twenty bags, which were duly

delivered on a wooden pallet and covered with a plastic tarp. Seeing this pile, I felt chagrined that I had perhaps over ordered and would have sufficient remaining to cement a bottom step to the porch, repair the cinder-block outdoor fireplace and point up the laid-stone foundation to the Camp as well.

I carried each eighty-pound bag of Sakrete (the wheelbarrow couldn't squeeze between the broad bottom step to the porch and a nearby birch tree) the 125 feet to the patio site, dumped it into an old galvanized washtub I found tucked under the Camp, and hand-mixed it with lake water. I was dumbfounded to discover just how little area it filled. Even when I added small rocks and pebbles from the lake bed and shore to fill up some of the larger cracks, I was dismayed to see how quickly a trowel full of cement would disappear between two rocks, as though the rocks themselves ate and digested the quantity of cement I fed them and still wanted more. I wound up ordering two more pallets of cement before I was done.

My grandfather, who was in his mid-sixties then and suffered a chronic bad back, often stood by, a satisfied look in his eye, and now and then pointed out a particular rock that would fit perfectly next to another. His unerring ability to accurately gauge those granitoid spatial relationships baffled me, but baffled or not, I was grateful for his suggestions.

"You work with rock long enough, Lad, you get a feel for it and a sight for it too."

Sometimes I'd pry, push, and shove a large boulder several feet to where I wanted it, only to discover that it was too high by a scant inch or two. This frustrated me to no end because it may have taken an hour or more to roll that one boulder into place only to find it barely poked its surface above the elevation string. If it was angular, I could sometimes smash off the offending nub with a sledgehammer, or sometimes I could wedge up an end and snake out smaller underlying rocks and then set it deeper. But that was seldom. Far too often they had to be moved aside to be used later in a different location. Nuts, again.

Even though Grandpa could no longer do "bull work," his mostly silent presence—excepting those infrequent jigsaw puzzle-like suggestions—was that of a co-worker and companion. We were doing this together. When a two or three-hundred pound boulder had to be set aside because it wouldn't fit, we both felt the frustration. In our own separate ways we both were pushing, tugging, cursing, and sweating, and when we finished two years later, leveling the last washtub of cement to cap the last section of the patio, we shook hands and smiled at each other at a job well done.

I believe it marks a milestone in a family relationship when a son (or grandson) first drinks alcohol with his parent. It's a graduation of sorts, a breaking of a barrier, a move toward greater equality and manhood. (It could also be for some, the first step off a cliff.)

My grandfather seldom drank. On New Year's Eve it was his custom to have a small whiskey in a large glass of ginger ale. That was the extent of his carousing. So after that last swipe of trowel on wet cement and firm celebratory handshake, it was with some trepidation that I went into the kitchen and returned with two Budweisers and offered him one. He looked at it for a moment, smiled slightly, and then swallowed a draft. "Thanks, lad, that was just what we needed."

I don't know if my grandma was aware of how much of a bonding experience the patio project became between my grandpa and me, but later that evening at the supper table, she said, "You know, dear, you two did such a good job with that patio, I wonder if next year you'd mind making it a little wider?"

PINE BRANCHES AND PRIVACY

The Camp was situated on a point of land that thrust into the lower end of the lake. A luxuriant mix of white pine and maple trees effectively screened that point from view. Grandpa referred to the latter as swamp maples. These differed from sugar maples, which were tall and majestic and in the fall had a bright yellow canopy, whereas the shorter and more slender swamp maples were spectacular in their sun-drenched scarlet, maroon and cardinal red. The soft forest green of the pines always seemed comforting as the susurrus whisperings of the breeze softly sifted through their needles, like a mother's breath to her babe sleeping in her arms.

The front of the Camp faced the main body of the lake. The patio had been built there for the view and afternoon sun. Behind the patio soared an ancient white pine, towering above the roofline. If one were boating down the lake, the Camp's location could be spotted over a mile away by that spire that stood head and shoulders above the surrounding tree tops. The lower branches swayed a scant three feet above the patio.

The two summers I had labored mightily to build the patio, pulled and pushed rocks, pried and levered boulders, sweated, grunted and groaned, Grandma would periodically visit the work site and admonish me to be careful of that venerable pine's branches, to just leave them be, and if they were constantly in the way of construction, well that was too bad, I'd have to put up with it. Grandpa silently nodded his concordance. And so the patio took a little longer than it would have otherwise, what with the constant ducking, dodging, and brushing aside of those heavy, needle-laden branches.

I'd carry Grandma's aluminum folding camp chair down to the level cement surface and she'd point to where she wanted it placed. She'd look at the lake, look at the chair's alignment, and carefully lower herself in the chair. Invariably it was strategically positioned so she could surreptitiously peer out onto the lake and view the passing boat traffic without being seen, or at least the top half of her not being seen - much like when a child covers his eyes and believes if he can't see you, then you can't see him.

When I asked what she was hiding from, she'd indignantly exclaim that she wasn't hiding from anything, she just liked her privacy. When I asked just what was so private about sitting on her own patio watching boats, she became flustered and said that it was nobody's business what she was doing, or what she was watching, or not watching. If she wanted to look at boats, then she'd look at boats and if she wanted to look at her newspaper, then that's what she'd do. She minded her own business, and she expected other people to do the same.

I recollected how, at home in Concord, if there was a noise or commotion heard in the street, she'd hustle to the front room window and carefully pull the white gauzy curtain aside just a crack so she could peek out without being seen. The inherent contradiction between her right to observe others versus her rights to privacy completely eluded her. Any attempt to amplify that hypocrisy was met with an acerbic, "Don't get smart with me, young man!"

She often launched into a monologue about when I grew older I would understand why certain things were for public consumption: what I did for a living, what state and town I lived in, the more illustrative members of the family genealogy, and the number and sex of one's offspring - if married. Forbidden revelations included how much money I made, how much I had in the bank, investments, "family" matters, nefarious and "black sheep" family members, and the usual religious and political preferences. These and many other topics of permissible and impermissible exposures to public scrutiny were pontificated upon, but in the end it seemed to me to all boil down to it was okay to know stuff about the other guy, but it was not okay for the other guy to know stuff about you - unless the information was favorable, or at least neutral.

Yup, Grandma was a gossip. She loved being in the know. She loved attention and she loved to brag about the family's accomplishments. With equal passion, she hated being embarrassed and was clearly swayed by what others thought. Her particular anathema to revelations about her financial affairs I think was fueled by two fires: one was her fear that we would be found wanting, that we didn't have enough, that somehow we were less than the Joneses. Second, after having gone through the Depression and having various down-and-out family members come to live with her and Grandpa until they could get back on their feet, that she would be taken advantage of or stuff would be taken from her. People knowing what you had made you vulnerable, and that was never good.

Grandpa, on the other hand, was just plain private. He believed it was nobody's business to know anything about him, period. He was perfectly content to go for hours without talking. Yet one of his favorite things to do was drive Grandma to a store to shop while he would sit in the car, smoke Camels, and watch people as they passed by. He was an inveterate people-watcher. He didn't particularly want to interact with them, he just wanted to observe. Sometimes he'd say to me, "Look at that man with the mustache. What do you suppose he does for a living?" I would look closely at the designated specimen and maybe venture a guess or pass with a noncommittal, "I don't know." And that could be the only utterance from Grandpa during the forty-minute wait for Grandma, who invariably had taken longer than she planned because she met Mrs. So-and-So, and they just had to catch up.

Both Grandma and Grandpa loved being outside on the patio, she, partially screened by the pine boughs and he, perched wherever there was an empty chair. She'd watch the lake traffic, read the paper, and comment on the local news. He watched the same lake traffic, smoked his Camels, and occasionally commented on the changing color hues on the opposite hillside or the way the wind riffled the water in some spots, but not in others. And the grand pine's lower branches drooped ever lower in the middle of this idyllic scene.

I craved the sun and openness and for two cents I would have sawed the damn branches off. Walking around them all the time was a bother. Grandma, sensing my antipathy toward them, commented every now and then that I was not to forget how much she liked those branches right where they were. They were like a tent which offered pseudo privacy and kept the sun off her - she was allergic to too much sun.

How the gods must have giggled the following year when they sent a spectacular nor'easter roaring down the lake with a drenching rain, three-foot white caps that crashed against our sea wall, lightning that blasted the eardrums and sent Grandma to bed with a pillow over her head, and a shrieking, lashing wind that caused the roof to leak in several new places, and yes, snapped two of the grand pine's lower branches.

One branch lay on the ground, leaving a two-foot jagged stump where the wind had wrenched it from the tree's trunk. The other branch had snapped three feet from the trunk and hung like a dead man from the gallows. The yellow-white of the splintered wood appeared like naked bones after a buzzard's feast. Lifeless green needles lay in the puddled water, their luster departed.

After the storm abated, Grandpa and I surveyed the carnage, a silent communion of sadness bound us together - as well as a frisson of apprehension of Grandma's reaction. After a long moment, he said quietly, "Get the saw, Lad."

Grandma recovered from her migraine late the following day. She usually had one whenever there was a thunderstorm at Camp. I thought her phobia of thunderstorms was the cause of her migraines, and to some degree I'm sure that contributed, but years later I learned that sharp, substantial changes in barometric pressure, which presage thunderstorms, often caused migraines in certain susceptible people.

She emerged from her bedroom, came downstairs and made herself a cup of tea. She always took it with milk and sugar. Wrapped in her pink bathrobe and scruffy slippers, she wandered out onto the porch overlooking the lake and the patio to check on the men-folk, meaning Grandpa and myself.

Grandpa and I had just finished trimming the grand pine's trunk where the branches had broken, cutting off the broken branch flush with the trunk. We dragged the boughs around to the back of the Camp with the intent of cutting them up later for firewood. The twigs and slash were dumped in the woods. We were coming up the steps to the porch when Grandma, having just registered what that gap in the tree screen that offered a broader view of the lake portended, emitted a shriek of incredulity, "Oh...Oh, my word...I don't believe this."

She put teacup and saucer down forcefully on the porch picnic table and trundled down the porch steps. Slamming the screen door behind her, she stomped down the five stone steps to the patio - usually she carefully picked her way down these same steps for fear of tripping and falling, but not today. Striding out onto the patio, she stepped in a path of full sunshine where there used to be shade and pointed at the two fresh scars on the grand pine, her forefinger quivering with emotion.

"Who did this?" she demanded and turned a malevolent glare to me first, then to Grandpa, then back to me - where it stayed.

"I want an answer, NOW," her voice grated between false teeth, her dewlap jiggling.

I tried to explain about the windstorm, the broken branches, how we couldn't leave the remains just lying there. Grandpa interjected quietly that he knew she was upset but it was no one's fault and he and the Lad had done what needed to be done...and we were all sorry about losing those branches. Words faltered, ceased, awkward silence descended.

Grandma, still fuming, whirled about and stamped her way back to the porch , saying, "Men! I have a headache and I'm going back to bed...You will just have to fend for yourselves today." The screen door slammed behind her.

THE DOCK

Building the patio gave me a fine sense of accomplishment, which was reinforced and expanded by the pleasure my grandparents took in spending time on it. There's nothing like reward to beget repetition. Consequently, I began to consider other projects at Camp. My grandmother's suggestion of extending the patio the following year was less than compelling. After all, the sweat from building the first one had barely dried on my skin. Plus, I wanted the idea to be my own.

I thought a deck off the living room had possibilities, but with a big L-shaped screened-in porch already in service, what was the point? Then I considered bringing in loads of loam, spreading it out to make a nice lawn - like one could play croquet on, but I wasn't sure how Grandma would take to that. The idea of putting in sliding glass doors off the living room wall to the porch occurred to me, but that didn't really fit with the Camp's rustic ambience. And then there was the additional problem of the Camp's laid stone foundation flexing with the spring thaws and winter freezings which would probably spring the rigid door casings.

One early morning I wandered out to the boat landing. The slowly spiraling tendrils of morning mist gradually burned off the lake as the sun rose higher in the eastern sky. I looked for the Sentry, the gray heron, but he wasn't there. Perhaps he'd come and gone already, his belly full of fish or frogs. The rowboat lay still in the water, its prow resting on an old tire covering the rocky shore. A length of chain ran from the bow to a swamp maple, securing it. As I stared at the boat, it hit me. A proper boat dock. That's what I could do for my next project.

Usually we laid two or three old car tires on the rocks at shoreline, pulled the rowboat's bow up onto them, and then tied it to the maple by the chain. For a couple years we used a makeshift, rickety, wooden dock that Grandpa and I cobbled together, but a surprise wind storm from the southeast had dashed that project to smithereens. A sturdy, wooden dock, long enough to dive off the end or cast a fishing line would be perfect. And it should be wide enough for a person to sunbathe on and still have enough room for another person to walk by.

About ten feet from the rowboat another boat was tethered to the shore, a thirteen foot aluminum Grumman with a ten horse-power Johnson motor that we used when we wanted to fish the upper end of the lake or spend a day at Wellington State Park. I supposed that could be tied up to the other side of the proposed dock. Then there were a couple of kayaks and the Sea Snark. Now everything didn't have to be tied up to the dock, but to get in and out of all these boats a dock would be handy. Obviously my project had to be expanded. A U-shaped dock, similar to what Mr. Irving had inside his boat house might fill the bill. On and on it went: planning, revision, expansion, revision again, material estimates, cost estimates, time tables, what would I need help with and from whom, and so on.

My Grandma asked, "You're awfully quiet, what's going on?"

"Just thinking about the dock."

My wife commented, "You haven't said a word in the past hour. Are you okay?"

"Just thinking about the dock."

Thinking about the dock morphed over time from actual planning to the post construction phase, the enjoyment of it. This took the form of reverie. It was pleasant. It was relaxing. It was a welcome distraction from stress. Captain Queeg had his little steel balls to fiddle with. Herbert Benson had his "relaxation response," others practiced yoga and meditation, and still others used drugs and alcohol - I had the Dock. Sometimes thoughts of the dock helped me through boring lectures. I pictured myself sliding from the dock into the Sea Snark or a kayak and heading out of the cove or spin casting from the dock's far end while the lecturer of the day droned on, the fan of his overhead projector providing a white-noise, soporific effect.

I have to admit that the dock also allowed a certain subterfuge, which I immediately rationalized as legitimate. To whit: I was pondering what Christmas presents my wife might like, when she suddenly loomed in my field of vision and demanded to know what I was thinking about - "The dock," I answered. Not all such answers were so benign.

I studied Martial Arts for a while. During vigorous warm-up exercises, in particular countless dozens of pushups, Sensei Johnson would intone, "Take yourself away from the pain and go to the beach. Picture the ocean, feel the water lapping at your feet, hear the seagulls, smell the salt air, put yourself there." Yup, the saltwater scene had nothing on the dock. As the lactic acid ache built up, I pounded nails in another plank of decking. As my muscles quivered and strained, I hoisted another four-by-four into position. Same principle, different venue.

I never did get to build that dock. Life and its vicissitudes intervened. And it's amazing how much I learned and how much I benefited from a project that never got off the ground.

SAILING

"So we beat on, boats against the current, borne
back ceaselessly into the past."
—F. Scott Fitzgerald, *The Great Gatsby.*

As far back as I can remember, I have always
loved being around water. I liked the look of it,
either in storm or stillness. I liked the feel of it on
my skin on a hot summer's day. I liked pulling my
way through it, either by rowboat, canoe or kayak.
But what I really wanted to do in water, and I had
not done, was learn to sail in it.

From early boyhood I had watched the Sailfish,
Sunfish, Sea Snarks, Cape Dories, O'Days,
Lightnings, Catamarans, and others sail past the
Camp. Sometimes they ghosted by on an
imperceptible breeze; other times they tore by in a
furious rush, heeled on gunwale by a gloriously
fierce wind. The very concept of mastering wind
and water, of playing with those two ubiquitous
elements to convey me where I wanted was a
siren's call that I had waited too long to answer.

Diagonally across the lake from our Camp was
a small marina, which rented out rowboats, canoes,
small aluminum outboard motorboats for fisherman,
and sailboats. The proprietor, Peter, a fit, tanned,
friendly man in his late thirties said he'd be happy
to give me sailing lessons. He said casually as I was
about to leave after having made arrangements for
my first lesson later that day, "Oh, yeah. You better

wear a bathing suit. You know, just in case."

Peter had been a math teacher at the local high school. He discovered early on in his short career that while he loved math, he wasn't crazy about teaching, especially teaching hormone-driven, emotionally labile teenagers. The second thing he loved, aside from his wife, was sailing. His wife, ever the pragmatist, and feeling his disillusionment deeply, persuaded him to spend the next five years teaching and saving every penny. She changed her part-time job to full-time to increase their income and savings. She said at the end of the five years if he still felt the same way about teaching, he would resign and with their savings they would either build or buy a small marina where he could be in and around the boats he loved so much. That arrangement lasted three years, whereupon they got a bank loan and bought the place. They had been in business now for ten years without a single regret.

A few hours later I was back, appropriately attired. Luckily, there was only a mild breeze, nothing to worry about. We mostly sat in a day-sailer a few hundred feet off shore while Peter explained and demonstrated how to tell wind direction, how to tack upwind, sail downwind and how the loudly-warned, "Coming about," could save a cracked skull. I learned about lines (not ropes) and luff, mainsheet, jib sheet, and spinnaker. Best yet, I actually made the craft do what I wanted it to do - sort of - some of the time. And I didn't tip us over.

On my fourth lesson out, there was a "brisk" breeze. I was running before the wind and attempted a controlled jibe to change direction back into the wind and before I knew it, the wind slammed into the sail, heeled us on edge so water ran over the gunwale, and then snatched the line out of my hand -- which was the only thing that saved us from capsizing. The boat righted itself and Peter roared with laughter. He was having a grand time. I sputtered an apology and he joked about the occupational hazards in his line of work.

Peter said he hadn't really worked since he left teaching. He had been at play ever since, all day long and every day--just playing. He said one should think hard and long about what they truly enjoyed doing and do that for a living. When the season ended for him here on the lake, he and his wife closed up for the winter and went to Florida, where he did exactly the same thing: rented boats, taught sailing, and it was all play.

I continued the lessons off and on through the summer--not so much out of necessity, for once one knows the rudiments of sailing the rest is just practice and refinement--but because I enjoyed his company and looked forward to our time together on the lake. More than once he waived the fee, saying it was on the house.

The Chiltons, a retired gentleman and his wife, had a tiny cottage hidden among the hemlocks across the cove from our Camp. He moored a Chris Craft in the cove - as well as a Cape Dory sailboat.

The Chiltons and my grandparents had known each other forever and whenever we passed them on the dirt road or met them at market in town, they always stopped and talked.

How Mr. Chilton learned of my newfound passion for sailing I never discovered, but it came to pass that on one of my afternoon treks to the mailbox - a half-mile to the main road - he stopped me at his driveway. He said that in a few weeks he would be needing to bring his sailboat ashore for the winter and store it in his shed. If I was willing to help him, I could use it in the meantime. I jumped at his offer. I never thought to ask him if he needed help with the Chris Craft as well.

His Cape Dory was a sixteen-foot beauty with a jib sail, main sail, and a fifty- pound center board. I don't know if the trim was teak or mahogany, but its polished, rich, warm color shone in the sunlight. The white gel coat gleamed and I felt proud to man the tiller. I had never sailed anything so grand. I lost count of how many times I took it out on the lake during those last remaining weeks, but a morning, afternoon, and early evening sail was common.

When it was time to drag it on rollers to the shed for winter storage, Mr. Chilton looked at me with a smile and said he guessed he'd be seeing me again in the spring. As I nodded my affirmation, I realized his eyes were the same shade of gray-blue as my grandpa's and they both wore the same kind of wire- rim glasses.

* * *

The next spring, shortly after I launched Mr. Chilton's Cape Dory, I was talking to Peter at the marina and he mentioned he was selling a Sea Snark. It was a tiny boat, about eight feet long with a lateen sail. Built of Styrofoam with a plastic skin, it held a maximum of 350 pounds. It rather looked like a small, dugout canoe with a sail.

Peter said most sail boat renters were couples, not too many singles, and they usually wanted a larger boat. I could have it at a reduced price. And so I became the proud owner of a bright, canary-yellow Sea Snark. I never sailed Mr. Chilton's Cape Dory again.

The name, "snark," intrigued me. A little research revealed that it was a word coined in 1876 by Lewis Carroll in his poem, "The Hunting of the Snark," and referred to a mysterious, imaginary animal. I thought that with such a heritage, my little Snark had a lot to live up to - and the sooner we got started the better.

The Sea Snark was a poor thing compared to the Cape Dory, but it was mine. For most of the summer, I sailed it as I had sailed Mr. Chilton's Cape Dory, in other words, most of the time. By summer's end I was rather proficient with that tiny boat. More than once I was the only boat out on that windswept lake when those with better sense stayed home and placed bets as to how soon I would capsize. I never did.

The thrill of heeling to the point where the gunwale's edge was an inch from taking water and the wind and spray and roiling white caps comprised my entire universe was addicting. It was an incredible summer. I felt seven feet tall and bullet proof.

* * *

It was a beautiful summer's day, a few small puffs of clouds and a moderate breeze blew from the west. Time for a quick sail before lunch. As the porch door closed behind me, Grandma's voice followed, "Be sure you're back for lunch. I know how you are when you're in that boat of yours. You lose all track of time."

Underscoring her admonition was Grandpa's quiet, but firm, "Mind the time, Lad."

I planned to take a straight shot crosswise to the wind, straight up the channel for a mile or so and then return the same way - an easy half-hour's run and fifteen minutes to spare. Indeed, it started out that way, running snappily across the water, the wind steady. Suddenly, without warning, I was going downwind, the small boat threatening to plunge its bow into the next wave. The wind had shifted from the west to the south and was now at my back. If this continued, I would have to tack all the way back, thus taking two to three times as long.

I let wind out of sail, came about, and began the now long slog home. The wind didn't shift again and so back and forth I zigzagged and with each turning closed distance incrementally. It wasn't long before I saw Grandpa standing on the patio, waving at me. I was late. I waved back, signaling that I understood.

Ten minutes later he was back. This time he whistled. I knew what that meant: I was in trouble. His whistle was famous in the family. For one thing, it was amazingly shrill. For another, it meant get here as fast as you possibly can cuz you're already in trouble and every second you take , you're in more trouble!

When you tack in sailing, you utilize an opposing force vector, the wind against another vector - the dagger board. The tiller provides the direction or angle. It's like a bullet ricocheting or similar to squeezing a wet, grapefruit seed between two fingers: it squirts out between the two forces. Two problems: when sailing at an angle into the wind, left than right but not directly into the wind, it's going to take at least twice as long. Heading more directly into the wind, results in a stall, all headway is lost and one has to start all over again.

I knew this. Grandpa didn't. My frantic tacking back and forth to get home as fast as I could, he saw as my playing around when I knew better - in blatant defiance of his whistle. And then, of course, the wind subsided. It didn't drop off entirely (my grandfather would have understood that), but instead of blowing, it half-heartedly puffed. So now I was tacking at half the speed. When I finally sailed into the swimming area, jumped overboard, lowered the sail, and dragged the Sea Snark up on the sea wall, I knew I was in for it. My grandpa was seldom angry with me, but when he was....!

I raced onto the porch where we ate in good weather. Cold tomato soup and a cold grilled cheese sandwich greeted me, and a note, "Gone to town. Be here when we return."

It was a very long two hours, I expect on a par with waiting a jury's verdict following a murder trial. When they finally drove into the yard, they emerged from their forest-green Pontiac, stony-faced, and avoiding eye contact. I went up to them and apologized for missing lunch and said I had come as fast as I could and started to explain about tacking.

"You can stop lying right there, son, before you make it worse for yourself. Your grandmother and I both watched you play in that boat of yours, even after I whistled. Don't try and tell me you hurried straight back, because you didn't. You just went back and forth and back and forth - and don't tell me you didn't."

I tried to explain again why I couldn't come straight back home, but he held up his hand as a policeman might stop traffic. "Stop. It's done. No more." He turned on heel and marched indignantly into the Camp, firmly believing I was self-centered, cavalier of their feelings and authority, and a bald-faced liar to boot.

That was my last sail of the season.

THE APPENDECTOMY

The war in Vietnam continued unabated and my training as a medic at Fort Sam Houston, Texas was coming to a close. My days were filled with training films, simulated exercises on dummies with rubber look-a-like wounds, and buddy-on-buddy practice drills. Night time dreams often contained scenes of bubbling, sucking, chest wounds, freshly charred flesh, eviscerated entrails hanging from gaping abdominal cavities, and similar depictions of carnage. These preoccupations were offset by frequent daydreams of floating on an inner tube in the middle of the cove on a tranquil summer's day at Camp or sleeping on the Camp's screened-in porch at night and hearing the bullfrog's serenade in the Little Frog Pond. The Camp was my refuge and sanctuary, both *in situ* and in fantasy. I couldn't wait to finish my training and return there.

After completing my training, an army buddy and I elected to drive from San Antonio, Texas to Concord, New Hampshire rather than use our paltry travel allotment on bus or train fare. Our only planned stop was at the Citadel, The Military College of South Carolina, where I attended my freshman year of college. The stop-over was for nostalgic reasons.

We managed to catch the traditional Friday afternoon parade. The Corps of Cadets in full-dress, blue-grey uniforms and stark-white webbing stood rigidly at attention as the battalion stretched arrow-straight along the far side of the field. Their brass gleamed and spit-shined shoes--polished until fingers ached- glistened in the South Carolina sun. An errant breeze from the nearby Ashley River fluttered the flags and guidons - all else was silent and motionless, a tableau frozen in time.

The stillness was shattered by the Battalion Commander's stentorian barked order, "PRESENT ARMS." Several hundred cadets brought up their M-1s in perfect two-count unison to the required position. The howitzer boomed and a puff of gray smoke erupted from the muzzle to hang in the air until the next Ashley River breeze swirled it away.

"ORDER ARMS." Again, in two-part harmony, M-1s were returned to their original position.

"PASS IN REVIEW." Band Company struck up a rousing martial air and the first company of the first battalion began to march, the drum's rataplan setting the cadence, the pronounced bass drum guiding the left heel strike, 120 beats per minute. Company by company they marched down the field, passed the reviewing stand, and returned to their crenellated barracks.

As we walked alongside the parade ground, it struck me how young the faces looked and I speculated how many of them would be shipped to Vietnam upon graduation and how many of those would wind up at Brook Army Medical Center in San Antonio where I had just left. Time at Camp looked better and better. The remainder of the trip home was uneventful.

Homecoming was wonderful: just holding my wife, having dinner with my grandparents, and sleeping in my own bed. But in truth it was all but a prologue to the main event--being at Camp.

The next morning we set out. The trip from Concord takes just under one hour, and paradoxically, in an abrupt turnabout from all the rush to get there, I drove slower than usual, savoring every landmark, relishing every familiar curve and straight-away on route 3-A. My wife had packed everything we needed except for perishables and we stopped in Bristol to purchase those. The First National hadn't changed a bit, even the checkout ladies were the same. After all, I had only been gone six months, but it seemed much longer. Familiarity gives a sense of security (and that too, is false in the long run). There had been something in my training as a medic against the ever-present background of war news and latest body counts and my tours through Brook Army Medical Center's Burn Unit and seeing G.I.s, no different than myself, burned and broken, that made having a sense of security very important to me.

We pulled into the Camp's circular driveway and I carried the groceries along the stone walkway to the door. I entered the kitchen and just stood a moment inhaling deeply the familiar admixture of kerosene from the kitchen stove, wood smoke from the Glenwood, pine needles from the two giant pines, and the ineffable mustiness of multigenerational age emanating from the very bones of the Camp. I was home.

We swam, lay in the sun, talked for hours, read the latest best sellers, probably ate and drank too much, and made our best effort at catching up on making love. The next few days were much the same as we became thoroughly immersed in reconnecting with each other before we returned to the quotidian demands of everyday life.

One evening, a little while after dinner, I began to experience sharp cramping in my abdomen, which after an hour became exigent diarrhea. I was thankful for the indoor plumbing that had replaced the outhouse a few years back. There came a brief hiatus in symptoms - just long enough to think the worst was over - and then came the worst: simultaneous vomiting and diarrhea of copious proportions. On my dash to the bathroom I grabbed a stew pot from the drying rack on the kitchen counter, which turned out to be a face-saving and mess-avoiding, just-in-the-neck-of-time maneuver. Evacuation and purging in synchrony keeps one busy. It also empties the gut quickly. However, being empty did nothing to alleviate the cramping. If anything, it worsened and seemed to focus in my right lower quadrant.

Due to the escalating war and constant demand for more warm bodies, my medic training had perforce focused on battlefield traumas and little on common dysfunctions of the body, but when my wife, who had left nurses training to have our babies, said, "You know, I think you're having an appendicitis attack and we ought to get you to the hospital," I intuitively knew she was right. The nearest hospital was in Plymouth, about ten miles away and she drove me there in record time.

Fortuitously, the Doctor on Call was a surgeon. When he learned that my wife had been in nurses training, he decided that the diagnostic process of determining whether I had appendicitis or something else would be an individualized education session for her. He reviewed the presenting complaints of nausea and vomiting, abdominal cramping, diarrhea, and tenderness in the right lower abdominal quadrant. Then he trailed a pair of metal clamps over the right side of my belly and then the left. The left quivered from the cold steel; the right remained rigid. Apparently that was pathognomonic for appendicitis as well. He pressed gently on each side, although it didn't feel all that gentle when he palpated the right. All this was accompanied with a running commentary to my wife, who appeared to be memorizing every word and action. She always was a good student. I was prepped and draped and wheeled into the operating room, hooked up to an I.V. drip, told to count backwards from one hundred, and by ninety-four I was out.

I woke up in the Recovery Room. A nurse told me everything went fine with the operation and I'd never have to worry about another appendicitis attack. They expected I should be up and walking around - albeit slowly and stiffly - within a day or two.

It didn't happen. Day two dawned and I was feeling wretched. I couldn't care less about their expectations. Day three was worse; when I wasn't feeling rotten, I was sleeping. I was running a fever on day four. The surgeon who had separated me from my appendix said I had developed an infection. I needn't worry, these things happen all the time. He was going to transfer me to the hospital in my home town.

On day five I was in the operating room in Concord Hospital, again draped and ready. A general anesthetic wasn't necessary, explained Dr. Carlson. A local was sufficient. He'd cut over the existing incision, remove most of the infection, put in a drain, and by tomorrow I'd be feeling much better and probably moving around, albeit slowly and stiffly. Like Yogi Berra said, "It's like *déjà vu* all over again."

I don't know what possessed me at the time, but I perked up and told him that I'd just returned from medic training and wanted to watch the procedure, if possible. He rolled his eyes, then smiled and said that could be arranged. The nurse brought in a large mirror, about the size of a medicine cabinet door. She placed it on a wheeled tray at the foot of the gurney and told me to indicate when she had it angled correctly so I could see my abdomen.

Dr. Carlson signaled he was about to begin and

asked if I was really sure I wanted to watch. I assured him I was. He shrugged, bent over, and sliced open my incision. He placed his hands on both sides of the open incision and pressed down. Immediately two cupfuls of yellow-green putrescence erupted from my abdomen, rather like a miniature volcano. My raised head flopped back on the pillow. I heard chuckles and snickers in the distance as I sank into darkness.

Two days later I was home and feeling better, except for some tenderness and stiffness around my incision. I walked slowly, noticeably bent over, and ever conscious of my stitches.

A couple weeks later, my wife came home from work and said that our experience with my appendix made her realize how much she wanted to be a nurse and it was time for her to return to school and finish her nurses training. I agreed....and asked if she wanted to go to Camp the following weekend.

KAYAKING: OR ANOTHER BOAT STORY

It began at Camp, my love of kayaking. It was an inauspicious beginning. Junior had come to Camp for the weekend and brought with him a red and white fiberglass kayak. It was a thirteen-foot long needle with a cockpit, a slalom boat designed for quick turns and darting, hummingbird-like maneuvers. As with a single-man scull, its stability resides not so much in the boat's design but in the motion of the craft and the proprioceptive reflexes of the paddler.

With a malevolent gleam in his eye, Junior invited Uncle Bob and me to try his kayak out. At first Uncle Bob demurred, but Junior persisted, goading him with the taunt of what kind of a sailor is afraid of a tiny boat that weighs less than he does. One might have thought that after a lifetime of such taunting, Uncle Bob would have learned to shrug and walk away, but such is the dynamic between first and second born sons that the "I dare you" gage evokes the "I'll show you" response every time - a hard-wired reflex buried stratums beneath the consciousness. Uncle Bob strode to the slender craft, grasped the edges of the cockpit with both hands, slid one leg inside, and gave a little hop to slide the rest of himself inside…and promptly capsized. Junior's mocking laughter bounced off the lake's surface. I noticed that even Grandpa smiled a little, but his was more a wry smile of commiseration, as though he had seen the same ploy many times before, differing only in the details. Junior turned to me and said, derisively, "And now it's your turn. Think you can do any better?"

I pulled the kayak into the shallows where the water was only a foot deep and straddled the boat. Sitting down in the cockpit's back edge, I slowly wiggled my legs into it. As I leaned out for the paddle, which Junior offered (just out of arm's reach), I felt the boat begin to slide under my right hip. I hurriedly shifted my weight to my left hip and the boat revolved in that direction. After several back and forths and a good deal of splashing, the kayak and I both quieted down and simply sat there in the water. I slowly began to paddle. I noticed a look of disappointment on Junior's face. I didn't go far, maybe five hundred feet, and cautiously turned around. I felt like a little old lady tottering on ice skates as I returned to the swimming area. Getting out of the kayak was as tricky as getting in, but I managed it without mishap. I resisted the urge to give Junior the raspberry.

I can't say that I enjoyed my inaugural paddle, but there was definitely some satisfaction in beating Junior at his own game. As I came up onto the patio, Uncle Bob slapped me on the back and said, "Good job, Pardner."

I didn't think about kayaks again until the following spring when Dartmouth's Ledyard Canoe Club sponsored the Mascoma White Water Races and the town of Hanover was suddenly inundated with cars buried under roof racks containing two, three, and four kayaks - single-man and two-man - of various colors. Some were sleek and pristine, others appeared as the walking wounded with bandages of gray duct tape and plasters of colorless, emergency fiberglassed repairs. Brilliantly hued life jackets and helmets were piled on back seats and double-bladed paddles protruded from car windows. It was like the circus had come to town.

I attended the races out of curiosity, finding a spot by the river's edge, just down from the single-lane bridge in Lebanon. I queried a wet-suited contestant—who appeared to be studying the river and its currents and eddies formed by rocks, some submerged and some not - as to what purpose were pairs of white poles suspended over the river by wires strung from trees on both banks. He explained that depending on the markings and colors on the poles (he called them gates), a kayaker had to go straight through them without touching or go to the left or right of them and then back up against the current. As he spoke, a cherry-red kayak sliced through the churning water towards us, executed a tight half-moon turn up through the gate, then another half-moon turn down river and he was gone, darting through the froth and standing waves like a dragon fly.

The vernal sun was warm; the spray from the rushing river was icy cold. The power of the raging water announced itself by assaulting the ears with a cascading thunder as it smashed against the banks and innumerable rocks. In the middle of the tumult these slender, fragile crafts leaped and flitted, spun and surged, and occasionally capsized. Those not successful at righting themselves by an Eskimo roll were thrown a life preserver on a rope. That was no water to be swimming in. It was glorious and I fell in love with the sport that afternoon.

Apparently the universe was paying attention and in a helping mood for a change because only a couple weeks later I heard of a Hanover High School teacher who was building his own kayak. Elements clicked and fell into place. I just knew I would join Mr. Merchant in building kayaks and become involved in the sport in a major way. And he appreciated the slave labor.

I spent countless hours after work and on weekends with Mr. Merchant that summer and fall shaping and sanding the plug, a solid model of a kayak from which a mold is made. Then more hours laying up the fiberglass sheets over the plug and slathering it with resin to make the molds, until at last we began to churn out kayak clones of white, yellow, blue, and red. "The Merchant Mold," as we dubbed it, was well used by the time he donated it to the Ledyard Canoe Club.

We also made our own paddles and neoprene spray skirts. I spent the winter in Dartmouth's smaller indoor pool learning the Eskimo roll. When spring came and the ice barely out, we were paddling the rivers, learning about currents, eddy lines, reverse hydraulics, and souse holes.

Serendipitously, Dartmouth College was at that time the Mecca for whitewater kayaking in the United States. Jay Evans, a former national champion and U.S. Olympic team coach was there, as was his son, Erik, the current national champion. Fritz Meyers, a national runner-up and international contender was also present. Tips, hints, advice, and coaching was the best available.

The movie, *Deliverance*, came out and two of my kayaking buddies and I decided to have an adventure and kayak the Chattooga, the river on which the movie was filmed. Is everyone familiar with the word hubris?

* * *

Don Wilson and Hans Carroll, my Hanover kayaking buddies, and I met Kay Swanson and Walt Blackadar at the Atlanta airport. On the drive from the airport to our motel in Clayton, Georgia, we became better acquainted. Both Don and Hans brought guitars. *Dueling Banjos*, the musical theme from *Deliverance*, was a foregone conclusion. However, neither performer was quite up to the rapidly escalating finger-picking and the duet collapsed amidst raucous laughter. Hans picked up with the haunting sounds of Cohen's *Suzanne*.

Suzanne takes you down to her place near the river

You can hear the boats go by…."

And thus, *Suzanne* became our own theme song

for our adventure, which we sang loudly and off-key at the slightest provocation.

"Walt already had established a reputation as a wild river runner and explorer. One sports magazine had called him "the king of kayakers" for his daring exploits on white water. Walt tried to downplay his fame with an "Oh, shucks, I'm just one of the guys" attitude. And in truth, he was a sincere and humble guy.

The Chattooga River flows along the border of South Carolina and Georgia. This pristine river is born in the North Carolina mountains and springs to life as it surges down their steep slopes, splashes over waterfalls, and swirls around bends and rock ledges until it empties 57 miles later into Georgia's Tugaloo lake. The *Deliverance* movie had made certain areas of the Chattooga popular; however, the whole river had not been well described and seldom run in its entirety--and we wanted to do just that. We gave ourselves three days to run it.

Day one of our expedition began by driving along a slender, one-track, woods road that gradually wound its way up the mountainside to Burl's Ford, a cramped pull-off where the river squeezed between its banks. A beat up, black Chevy sedan sat arrogantly in the middle of the pull-off, preventing any other vehicle from parking or turning around. Our two station wagons, roof racks laden with kayaks and paddles, slowed to a stop, indicating our intent to park and unload.

The Chevy doors opened and disgorged two

good old boys dressed alike in jeans and white T-shirts with sleeves rolled up on their shoulders. A cigarette dangled from the mouth of one; the other held a Mason jar of clear liquid.

"Whatch'all doin here?" drawled the one with the cigarette, belligerence and challenge glinting in his eyes.

The Chevy's back window rolled down to reveal two young women, one with a blond page boy, the other with shoulder-length chestnut hair, both having eyes bright with curiosity...and something else. Perhaps anticipation?

"Hi, there," Don Wilson greeted them with a disarming smile. "We're from up north and came down here hoping to put our boats in and kayak a piece of the river."

"Up north, huh. You don't wanna be boatin' this part of the river," said the one with the Mason jar. He took a swig from the jar and gave a little shudder as his Adam's apple bobbed up and down with the swallow. "Y'all git kilt."

"Here," he offered the Mason jar to me. "Have some shine." His expression suggested the gesture was more dare than generosity. Having heard stories of going blind from moonshine as well as suffering other neurological and gastrointestinal disorders, I declined, saying it was too early for me.

His face tightened. His shoulders squared. "You northern boys too good to share a drink with us?" He took a step closer. The one with the cigarette moved forward in unison.

Hans, instantly sizing up the situation, smoothly intervened. "What he's not fessing up to is that he tied one on last night and has one hell of a hangover and just the smell of booze will probably make him chuck…but I don't mind having his share," and he held out his hand for the jar.

Appeased by this fiction and expression of goodwill, the two young men visibly relaxed and a conversation ensued as to where the killer thirty-foot waterfall was located on this section of the river. A few minutes later they were helping us offload boats and carrying them to the river's edge. I remember wishing that all threatening situations would resolve as readily.

Here the river was narrow, dropping fast over ledges and rushing through rock-bound chutes and flumes. Steel-tipped paddle blades screeched against stone as braces were hastily employed to make the next turn, avoid a barely submerged boulder, or line up one's craft for the next drop. At the bottom of most drops lay a pool or run-out where recovery could be made from a spill or faulty Eskimo Roll. The absence of such a pool could make life difficult.

However, it was in one of these gentle runouts that Walt inexplicably turned over and failed to right himself with an Eskimo Roll. After three attempts, he bailed out and swam his boat ashore. We couldn't resist the tease and in unison (but little harmony) we bellowed, "Walter, row your boat ashore." I thought even Peter, Paul and Mary might get a chuckle out of the situation.

As Walt emptied water out of his boat, I pondered this incident. There was no reason for Walt to have tipped over and his roll was nearly infallible. I wondered if it was his way of leveling the playing field, a way of minimizing his reputation to promote bonding with us.

After several stops to scout out what we thought might be the waterfall, we heard a rumbling roar in the distance that left no doubt in our minds that we were almost there. A hasty paddle to shore and out of our boats to see what was there. Forty feet across and thirty feet down the waterfall tumbled and cascaded with a booming crash that reverberated back from the hillsides. It was magnificent and awesome, and completely unrunnable due to a bulge halfway down its face which would crush the spine of both kayak and rider. We paused awhile to dry out in the sun's warmth and then began the treacherous portage along the spray-slippery rocks beside the falls.

A mile farther and the Chattooga narrowed again and we soon came to a five-foot ledge where the only decent passage was in the middle. The heavy spring runoff from two weeks ago had left a tree draped across the two boulders framing the entrance, rather like a natural bridge -- or a portal tomb. With little room to spare overhead or to the sides, we managed to hit the opening dead center, ducked low under the tree and shot over the ledge's lip, like water out of a squirt gun.

The river narrowed even more; the bare rock of the hillsides plunged straight down into water, making stopping and scouting often difficult and occasionally impossible. The water picked up speed and paddling became unnecessary except for change of course and bracing as eddy lines were crossed. Abruptly, the river ahead of us dropped out of sight and a mist appeared in the air above the lost horizon line. We paddled with all our might for shore, managing to find a sliver of flat ledge where we disembarked. A hazardous scouting along the rocky slopes showed us that the river became squeezed into a torrential chute of foaming, churning wild water for three hundred yards and dropping about forty feet in elevation. It was like a long, slender waterfall where a flip would be disastrous. Only Walt and Kay dared to run this one. Walt charged down this ribbon of white froth like a bronco buster on a wild stallion. Then came Kay. Half way down he suddenly flipped toward the rock wall bounding the side of the chute. The canyon echoed back the screech of his metal-tipped blade as he tried to take a brace off the rock wall. With his body half submerged and half out of his boat, he made a final stab at the canyon wall and up he came to finish the run as though nothing had happened.

We camped that night on a sandbar. The air-filled flotation bags that we pulled out of our kayaks did double duty as storage bags for our food, bedding, and clothes. Everything in the bags was damp from our exhalations that had filled them. The tent pegs kept sliding out of the sand and the tents sagged in the middle, threatening to collapse altogether. However, the excitement of the adventure and our burgeoning camaraderie far outweighed the small glitches along the way. We swapped stories around the fire and drank too much of Walt's "dragon juice." We awoke the next morning to chilly air and semi-frozen toothpaste.

Day two was planned as a twenty mile paddle covering sections two and three. The second section was exceptionally pretty as the Chattooga gradually worked its way down in elevation. Tranquil farmlands lay on either side as we drifted by.

Section three brought more excitement. Soon we came to the Rock Garden, a spot where great arching blades of granite erupted out of the river bed like dinosaur's teeth, hungry and carnivorous. The atmosphere seemed prehistoric and frozen in time.

A few bends in the river later brought us to Five Finger Falls, a lovely, tumbling cascade that drops lightly into the river. This waterfall also signaled that we were practically on top of Dick's Creek, a six-foot drop spanning the breadth of the river. At low water level one can paddle right to the lip where bare rock is exposed, step out, climb down, and lift the kayak over and down. However, at high water level one has either to barrel straight over or make an almost impossible portage on the left bank. We barreled straight over.

The sun was past the meridian and our

stomachs were rumbling. We pulled out of the river in a quiet little setback and eagerly rummaged through our storage containers for food. Lunch consisted of gorp, Kool-Aid, and venison jerky -- the latter compliments of Kay's last hunting trip in Montana.

The Narrows lay ahead. They were just that -- a narrow, rock-walled canyon with three drops in succession, standing waves three to four feet high, and tricky, switchy currents. Half way down Don suddenly flipped, and before he could roll up, the surging currents had wrenched him out of his boat, along with his bow flotation bag. The bow of his boat immediately filled with water, and, stern up, it bobbed and bounced down the last stretches of the Narrows. Walt and Hans came to Don's rescue, while Kay tried to rescue the boat. As I turned my head to see what was happening, over I went. Four times I tried to roll and each time was slapped down by the boiling currents. Finally I bailed out, crawled on top of my overturned boat, and rode out the remainder of the Narrows in this fashion.

Then came the Roller Coaster. Appropriately named, it was an extended series of large standing waves. In the high water we were in, they were between four to five feet in height -- huge slanting hills of white, churning, solid water, not very dangerous and just plain fun. It didn't last nearly long enough.

Section three ended at a nasty, man-eating, waterfall named Bull Sluice—a ten-foot drop where the Chattooga roars over the fall, crashes at the bottom, and then leaps backward onto itself in a seething reverse hydraulic. Reportedly, several people have drowned here, some by overturning and becoming caught in the "Keeper" at the bottom, turning over and over helplessly. The keeper is formed when large chunks of the lip break off, drop to the bottom, and roll a couple of yards forward. The water then hits these boulders and is forced up and backwards and thus a circular motion is created -- a keeper, or reverse hydraulic. Claude Terry, a river guide, said he had seen a raft caught in Bull Sluice's keeper for over an hour. He never mentioned what happened to the paddlers.

Don, Hans, and I unanimously agreed to walk around this one while Walt and Kay girded their loins (or spray skirts) to go in over the horns of the Bull. We watched apprehensively from our riverbank perch beside the lip as Walt approached warily, then committed himself to the current. His red kayak shot over the left edge, plunged down, and suddenly jolted to a momentary halt as he crunched into a submerged ledge halfway down. Sliding off, he hurtled the remaining five feet into the churning cauldron below. Driving his paddle deeply into the white froth in an attempt to find more solid water beneath, Walt muscled his kayak through the back-lashing river to safety. Kay's run was almost identical to Walt's. A quarter mile later, we took the kayaks out at a sandy beach on the left bank. We'd had enough for one day.

The fourth and last section of the Chattooga has been called the worst (or best) the river has to offer. It has some spectacular whitewater. What I remember most is almost drowning.

Corkscrew. True to its name, Corkscrew curves left, surges right, drives left, piles to the right, and so forth, until it dumps into another small, fast-moving pool. Before you can catch a breath, you're at "Crack in the Rock," a narrow split in a dam-like ledge spanning the river where the Chattooga squirts through with tremendous force into another pool. The remaining two rapids are practically contiguous so that the actual difficulty is magnified: Jawbone and Sock'Em Dog. The first is a long eight-foot chute, followed by two quick twists to the latter, an eighteen -foot free fall dumping into a churning, boiling mass of horrendous looking water.

We prudently decided to run only the first fall and portage the rest. Don and I would take an assault raft; the others would be in their kayaks. The kayaks would take the lead over the first fall, pull out, and stand by with a safety rope for the raft, just in case Don and I couldn't bully the unwieldy raft ashore in time. The kayaks made it and Hans, Walt, and Kay stood on shore, waiting. Don and I grinned at each other and pushed off.

As we approached the lip of the drop, the current abruptly swung us around backwards. There was a weird backward falling sensation, a roaring in our ears, and then cold water all around. The raft flipped over and we swam desperately around in

that churning froth, trying to discover the surface.
Our Flotherchock life vests were practically useless
in that super aerated water.

When we surfaced, Don struck out for shore,
and stupidly I grabbed for the raft. Before I realized
my mistake, the raft and I were swept out of that
tiny pool and toward the entrance to Corkscrew. By
this time I knew it was too late to try to swim to
safety. I had to stay with the raft, wherever the
lashing current drove it.

Meanwhile, Don had reached shore, and he and
the others were struggling over the spray-slippery
rocks with the rope, trying vainly to catch up with
me. The ride through Corkscrew was terrifying, my
strongest memory being of clenching the assault
raft's safety lines as hard as I could, my body strung
out behind in the turbulent water like a fishing lure.
Sometimes I banged into submerged rocks,
sometimes I glanced off them, and infrequently I
would miss one or two. (Without my quarter-inch
wet suit, I'm sure I would have been a bloody,
lacerated mess. Luckily, all I received were
substantial multi-colored bruises.) Sweeping out of
corkscrew, I tried to swim the raft ashore before I
hit Crack in the Rock. I didn't make it. I think if I
had left the raft I would have made it, but I couldn't
bring myself to let go of the only thing in the
Chattooga that was floating.

Crack in the Rock was so narrow I thought the
raft would get wedged in its narrow V, but the
force of the water scraped us right through. In the

short interval between there and Jawbone, I knew I couldn't swim to shore, but maybe I could pull myself into the raft. Filled with determination I pulled, wiggled, and squirmed--but I didn't quite make it. I swirled into Jawbone and down its eight-foot chute. Before I could appreciate the fact that I had successfully flushed down that drop, I shot out into thin air and hurtled down eighteen feet into the ugliest hole I've ever seen. The raft and I slammed into the huge standing wave just out from the bottom. The safety lines were slapped out of my clenched fists, and I was tossed, turned, dragged along the bottom, only to be tossed back under the wave again. I remember thinking, *"So this is how I'm going to die. There's no getting out of this one."* I felt fatalistic and resigned to the outcome.

And then I remembered I had read that in this reverse hydraulic situation, one should swim to the bottom (where the current was less), swim to the obstruction causing the reversal current (usually boulders), get over the obstruction to the downriver side, and then head for the surface. Finding the bottom when you're being turned over and over is difficult. I found it by luck. Which way was the obstruction? No time to ponder, just go for it. Almost out of breath. Feeling desperate. My feet touch something. Bottom? Kick down hard just as I can't hold my breath any longer -- and my face breaks into open air and I gasp in froth and begin choking. I'm alive. Weakly, I swam over to a bobbing log, draped myself over it, still choking and coughing, and waited for the others to catch up. I was surprised to be alive--and grateful. The appreciation of being alive after believing I was going to die was a singularly unique and ineffable experience.

The rest of our expedition was anticlimactic. After a few more minor rapids and a few more miles we reached Tugaloo Lake and the takeout point on the South Carolina side. A picnic area bordered the boat ramp. A young family gathered around a table. A woman stood apart at an iron railing by the lake, smoking a cigarette. I approached her and asked if she could spare a smoke (I stopped smoking two years previously). It was a celebration of being alive.

When we arrived at the motel, Hans asked how I was doing and could he do anything for me. I asked if he'd be willing to play *Suzanne* for me. He did.

"And Jesus was a sailor

When he walked upon the water...."

When Hans left the room, he paused and said, "Next time you go kayaking, you better wear your Jesus shoes."

The next day we parted: Walt to Idaho and his beloved Salmon River, Kay to Montana, Don, Hans, and I to New Hampshire and Vermont, each carrying his own memories. These have been mine.

* * *

Shortly after my return from our Chattooga adventure, I was back at Camp sitting in my kayak in the placid, translucent waters of the cove. Sitting close to me in another kayak I had made from the Merchant Mold was Billy, a scrawny, good-natured teenager and a cousin by marriage. We were discussing my next proposed adventure—ocean kayaking from Portsmouth Harbor to the Isles of Shoals, ten miles off the coast—when he asked me what would I do if I capsized and couldn't pull off an Eskimo roll. "It's a real long swim, you know," he chuckled.

Billy's question plagued me for the rest of the day. It was a very pragmatic question and I couldn't help but remember the occasions on the Chattooga and other rivers that I had tipped over and my trusty roll had failed. Yes, I had better find a solution to that little problem. I suppose if worse came to worst we could always have a rescue boat shadow us, but that took all the adventure out of it as well as nullifying the challenge.

By late afternoon I thought I had the answer. I asked Billy to jump in his kayak and join me in the cove. We paddled out to the middle where I deliberately tipped over and bailed out. While treading water next to my boat, I quickly flipped it back upright. There was only a negligible amount of water sloshing around inside. I asked Billy to bring his kayak parallel and proximate to mine, bow to bow and stern to stern. Then he placed his paddle and mine crossways on top of the boats, one paddle in front of both cockpits, the other paddle behind the cockpits. He held tightly to the paddle ends on his boat while I grasped the ends that overhung the outside edge of mine. Holding the paddles, one in each hand, I simply lifted myself out of the water and slipped inside the cockpit of my kayak. It was easy and it worked. The only caveats were that one had a partner and he had both paddles available. Later, I tried this method in white water and it was still workable, although swirling currents and half-submerged rocks increased the challenge. For ocean travel it would be just fine. I began planning my ocean kayaking adventure.

One fallout from my Chattooga adventure was that I returned not humbled by almost being eaten by the river, but instead filled with hubris, ten feet tall and bulletproof. One would have thought--or hoped--that any normal, reasonable person having a near-death experience would have developed a modicum of caution. But no. We began running rivers almost every weekend in Maine, New Hampshire, and Vermont. I probably would have drowned sooner or later except for a trip down the Pemigewassette at flood level.

Racing down the river, we came to a point where there was a waterfall. At the bottom, the river abruptly turned to the right forming a dog leg. The trick was to move close to the right bank, power off the waterfall, and while in the air take a right paddle brace off a large flat-topped boulder, swivel one's hips to the left and thus swing the boat to the right, and drop down pretty as you please, perfectly aligned in the dog leg—except, a split second into the paddle brace my right shoulder dislocated. Paddling with just one hand in white water was a joke and it took me awhile to struggle to shore. I was lying on the ground cursing when my physician-friend-kayak-buddy, Don Wilson, came ashore and took my injured arm in both of his hands, stuck his foot in my armpit and pulled. I remember screaming loudly as my joint realigned.

Later, I learned that in addition to the dislocation I had also done damage to the deltoid muscle and ripped the bursal sac. I was in a sling for several weeks. And that is what it took to squash my hubris and curb my white water adventures: not almost drowning, but the combination of lots of pain that persisted for several weeks whenever I moved my arm, and damage to my body that persisted even longer. Later on, a bout of delayed PTSD reinforced that change…and I never did kayak to the Isle of Shoals.

I returned to Camp where my interest in kayaking had begun. My arm was still in a sling and I was still recuperating. I couldn't row a boat, I couldn't sail, and I couldn't paddle. I settled into a chaise lounge on the screened porch that overlooked the patio and the swimming area, and I began to write about kayaking, boats, and Camp.

REPRESSION

My neighbor stepped on a nail while roofing his garage and I sat in a Dartmouth-Hitchcock Medical Center reception area waiting for him to hobble out for a ride home. I selected a *Dartmouth Alumni Magazine* to read over several *Good Housekeeping*s and *Woman's Day*s. As I scanned the table of contents, a kayaking article caught my eye. The story described the last adventure of an intrepid kayaker on a solo trip on the South Fork of the Payette River in Idaho. Somehow he became entangled in the branches underneath a tree (grimly called a "strainer") spanning the river's channel.

Perhaps -- knowing he couldn't paddle over or around the tree -- he thought by intentionally flipping over he could slide under it. There was no question of having to paddle, the force of the wild water was more than strong enough to drive him under the tree to the other side -- unless there were branches on the underside. There were...and he became ensnared and drowned.

When he didn't return, a search party embarked on a rescue mission. His body was found and brought home. His friends returned the following year to fasten a bronze plaque commemorating him on a boulder near where he died.

I decided to keep the article to read more thoroughly later. Later turned out to be next year on summer vacation at Camp. While rummaging through a cardboard box filled with articles, journals, and other readings I'd come across the aforementioned story and began reading.

Within just a few sentences my breath caught in my throat, my eyes bugged out, and I felt as though my heart seized up. The words jumped off the page and slapped my face, demanding attention--WALT BLACKADAR. The kayaker being described was Walt, my kayaking buddy from our Chattooga adventure. A year ago, when I initially read the article, my mind blocked me from recognizing Walt's name. I had read the whole thing and it just never registered.

I stood there on the screened porch, dumbstruck and speechless. I still couldn't quite believe my eyes. I read the article a third time to make sure my mind wasn't still playing tricks…and perhaps it was because I thought I heard, faintly echoing in the distance, the haunting lyrics:

Now Suzanne takes your hand
And she leads you to the river/
And she lets the river answer
That you've always been her lover

And then my vision became blurry as I mourned the passing of my friend.

PTSD

Walt's death affected me profoundly. His drowning and my near drowning preoccupied my thoughts. I wondered if he felt as I had (resigned) or if he raged against the approach of that "good night." I tried to avoid thinking in that direction, but I couldn't let go of it. These thoughts, like Poe's *Imp of the Perverse*, held me in a morbid obsession.

One day, as I pictured Walt trapped underwater in those tree branches -- like skeletal hands clutching his body in a death grip -- lungs screaming for air and being unable to suppress that inevitable, fatal gasp -- I realized I was holding my own breath and heard in my own ears a roaring tumult of roiling water that wasn't there. What I saw was not what was before my eyes, but the blurry swirl of a river's gorge. The cold, silty taste of river water filled my mouth.

My first flashback left me shaken. After several years of considering my Chattooga experience to be but fodder for story-telling and bragging rights, now I was unwillingly held hostage to reliving it. A few days later, I had another flashback, then another.

Then the nightmares started. They didn't occur on any regular basis, and not all that often -- just often enough so when I went to bed, I wondered if I would sleep the night through or if it would be one of "those" nights. It didn't take long for me to discover that when a nightmare did happen, the best thing for me to do was to get out of bed and engage my mind in something else -- usually accompanied by a snack. Unlike regular dreams, which evanesced soon after awakening, these nightmares tended to hang around for a while, unless I could focus on something interesting. Sometimes it was late night TV, sometimes it was the news, but most often it was physical exercise where the focus was riveted on the number of sets and repetitions -- and effort. Max weight on the last rep worked the best of anything to shake off the nightmare.

The flashbacks sometimes erupted out of the blue with no apparent precipitant, and other times they were triggered by obsessive thoughts. And sometimes they were caused by visual stimuli.

One evening, my two sons and I were watching the movie, *Das Boot*, and an underwater shot of the submarine had me, in the wink of an eye, holding my breath and straining my head upwards, as though desperately searching for the surface. I gripped the arms of my recliner so hard it's a wonder I didn't rip the arms off. I got up and went into the kitchen to surreptitiously recover.

Similarly, a couple of auditory triggers were guaranteed to instantly transport me into the Chattooga's maelstrom, namely a bar or two of "Dueling Banjos" or "Suzanne." Fortunately, their popularity waned over the past few years and consequently they were not heard that often.

I stopped swimming in water that was over my head. I no longer dove in -- I walked in. I avoided having my head under water. This was driven home to me when I went to the Florida beaches on vacation. In the past, when the waves were rolling in, I would swim out and body surf them. Now the idea of being enveloped by the roiling turbulence was enough to make me hold my breath, turn my back, and look for high ground. Waves that once upon a time I would have delighted in, were now ominous and full-bellied with malevolence.

This new feeling of vulnerability was maddening and debilitating. The feeling of not being in control was anathema. I had been scared in the past, but I always functioned. This sensation of panicky susceptibility could not stand. I had to do something about it.

I began a program of counter phobic measures, beginning with one of my triggers -- movies of underwater scenes. These were usually war movies featuring submarines. I sat on the sofa, did deep breathing and progressive muscle relaxation exercises until I felt deeply relaxed. Then I watched *Crimson Tide, the Guardian* and even *Das Boot* over and over. *The Perfect Storm* was particularly challenging. I saw reruns of Lloyd Bridges in *Sea Hunt* and documentaries with Jacques and Philippe Cousteau. The repetition paired with the relaxation helped. At this stage, it was more important to focus on retraining the physical response.

I wrote out scenarios in which I swam increasing distances in the cove, then kayaked the same distances, then practiced the Eskimo Roll. I discovered that with greater immersion in these activities came less adverse reaction. If I goofed off for several days, the fear response insidiously wormed its way back. Frequent, graduated exposure coupled with positive self-feedback was the answer for me -- first in imagination, then followed by the actual experience. Incremental progression was important. Taking too big a bite could cause a setback. Positive self-talk centered on a realistic appraisal of progress made also proved helpful.

I played "Dueling Banjos" and "Suzanne" endlessly until they lost all meaning like a child says a word over and over until it makes no sense.

I tried EMDR (Eye Movement Desensitization and Reprocessing) for a while with a Psychologist friend, but it didn't seem all that different from what I was doing on my own. Nonetheless, I appreciated his sincerity in trying to help.

It took less than a year to overcome the dysfunction. Now, I dive into water. I swim over deep water. I kayak and play in the waves in the lake. I'm not interested in doing whitewater anymore, but I enjoy watching it. However, I still have the occasional flashback--more like a memory flash--but it's mild and only elicits a mild tension, a gentle reminder of erstwhile kayaking buddies, the darker side of adventures, and the dangers of hubris.

GRANDMA AND JACK AND MLK AND....

Grandma was a woman of strong opinions and there was very little she didn't have an opinion about. Additionally, she believed that she should share her opinions with those around her, whether they agreed with her or not, and whether or not they even listened. To not express her opinion was akin to leaving food on one's plate—wasteful, unnatural, and morally dubious. How she came to her opinions, I don't know. I surmise many were based on what was politically correct at the time. Other opinions may have been inculcated from her family of origin, friends, and neighbors. Few, I think, were products of her own critical thinking because on those occasions in which I asked for an explanation, I received such comments as, "You'll understand when you're older" or "That's just the way some things are."

One of my Grandmother's firm opinions was that ladies did not engage in physical exertion. Of course that exempted such chores commonly construed as "women's work," such as hours spent on her feet cooking, cleaning, making up beds, shopping, and so on. Men's work, or "heavy work," comprised such activities as shoveling snow off sidewalks and porch roofs or coal into furnaces, moving furniture, spading the garden, changing storm windows, and so on. But it wasn't quite that simple.

Exercise for the pure joy of it was the province

of children and teenagers, but not acceptable for adults. Hours spent repairing the dirt road at Camp - digging out and moving boulders, filling in ruts, knocking down crowns, trundling wheelbarrows laden with dirt and rock - was men's work. Grown men playing football, baseball, basketball, or similar sport she saw as a regression to childhood and unseemly.

When I was in high school, Jack Lalane, fitness guru, was a regular feature on television. Good-looking and personable, he exuded strength and vitality; in his mid-forties he looked twenty years younger. He cajoled those in TV land to exercise along with him. While I thought him an effective proselytizer of the benefits of regular exercise, Grandma thought he was asinine. She couldn't imagine why a grown man would choose to huff and puff doing pushups like a teenager when he should be spending his time holding down a regular job - completely oblivious to the fact that Jack was making a pretty penny doing what he loved.

Jack died recently at the age of ninety-six, hale and hearty to the very end. On the other hand, Grandma, who adamantly disavowed the value of exercise for its own sake and bragged that she had outlived three of her family doctors, lived to the same age as Jack. To be fair to Jack, Grandma's last few years were spent mostly bedridden, in ill health, and riddled with pain from severe osteoporosis and resulting fractures of her vertebrae (if she had but followed Jack's advice and partaken of some regular bouts of exercise, those old bones would have been denser and stronger, but that's rubbing the proverbial salt in the wound). Both Grandma and Jack were of strong opinions.

I took up running in my mid-thirties and continued for three decades. I remember one occasion when I brought Grandma to Camp: she was sitting on the patio in the shade of the giant white pine chatting with my wife and watching boat traffic. I was preparing for a run and was wearing a T-shirt earned in a recent marathon. Grandma peered at the inscription, gold lettering upon a maroon background - "Hickory Ridge Marathon "- and audibly sniffed. I ignored her provocation and resolutely embarked on my standard six-mile run. It was a hot, sunny August afternoon. The road paralleled the shoreline of the lake for three miles and then veered away, at which point I turned around and headed back to Camp. I returned hot, sweat-soaked, and feeling my post workout achy glow. I stripped off my T-shirt, running shoes, and plunged into the lake. I surfaced and just hung there, suspended, weightless, reveling in the delicious coolness enveloping me and feeling the heat of my body dissipate. It was remarkably sensuous and relaxing. I heard Grandma sputter to my wife, "I'll never understand why he does that to himself. It can't possibly be good for him. Did you see him when he took off that shirt, all hot and sweaty like that. I swear he'll give himself a heart attack."

* * *

Prejudice as a noun is a preconceived opinion, its depth and scope limited only by the emotional intensity of its owner. When I was in high school, Concord, New Hampshire boasted a population of 25,000. It had one black family, the Bacons. At that time the vogue word was, "colored." For a state capital, Concord was rather insular. The Bacons kept to themselves. I never saw them. Grandma would occasionally refer to them, not in any pejorative way, but as one would mention a curiosity.

Rosa Parks crossed the Rubicon and Grandma said not a word, perhaps she didn't notice. The news of the Kent State killings splashed across the country, if not the world. Even Grandma couldn't ignore that. While she didn't think it right for students to be causing a ruckus - after all, their parents were spending their hard-earned money for them to get an education, not cause riots - it was downright wrong for our soldiers to be shooting our own children.

But before Kent State, Martin Luther King began to take up more space and air-time in the national news and his name became associated with civil unrest, disharmony, and riots. MLK was arrested and jailed. Anyone serving jail time couldn't possibly be up to any good (completely disregarding such jailbirds as Mahatma Ghandi,

Nelson Mandela, Siddhartha, and so on). His "I have a dream" speech caught the nation's ear and became a rallying cry. Grandma perceived it as a war cry, a source of more dissension and discontent. She had him pegged as a rabble-rouser. She never addressed the race issue in general or integration in particular, but she made no bones about the fact that she thoroughly disapproved of anyone who split the country apart and turned people against each other (following that logic, I suppose she would have taken umbrage with George Washington, Abraham Lincoln, and FDR, but she never uttered a word about those personages).

In retrospect, I think the root of Grandma's antipathy towards MLK was not race after all, but rather about her need for control. It was clear that Grandma ran the roost at home; she needed to feel in charge. Not having a firm grip on the reins allowed chaos to reign and that was anathema to Grandma. In her mind, MLK was associated with chaos. Where there was strife, there he was speechifying. I don't think she ever bothered to sort out cause from effect or action from reaction. He was in the thick of it and that was enough for her: guilt by association. "You are who you associate with was one of her favorite aphorisms. How such a man could be awarded the Nobel Peace Prize was way beyond her.

The assassination of MLK in 1968 offered no relief to Grandma's disgruntlement, for instead of the expected cessation from discord there now came a clamoring campaign to honor his efforts and memory by creating a federal holiday of his birthday. Much to her satisfaction, there was substantial disagreement over this. Even President Reagan expressed a disinclination to support such a measure. However, her satisfaction was short-lived as the U.S. Senate finally passed the bill by a substantial margin. President Reagan bowed to political pressure and in 1983 signed off, saying, "since Congress seemed bent on making it a national holiday...."

That was on the federal level. On the state level it was a different matter. Several states were not so inclined to accede. Nevertheless, as time passed and a growing consciousness over civil rights permeated America's collective thinking, one by one the hold-out states entered the fold - except for Arizona and New Hampshire. While Grandma's faith in all things governmental was badly shaken, at least her granite state showed clear thinking. Several times the state's legislature had voted down the motion, and each time Grandma cheered their wisdom. Each rejection validated her opinion. But eventually, in 1999, New Hampshire had the dubious distinction of being the last state in the Union to officially recognize MLK's birthday. She was crushed. Grandma attributed such misguided decision-making to all those young whipper-snappers who had been elected to the legislature. Well, they wouldn't last long.

* * *

Concurrent with MLK's all too frequent headlines was the 1961 presidential election. John F. Kennedy was running and he was - Catholic. Grandma was in a fret. She thought JFK was smart, personable, and well-qualified. She liked him - but there was that Catholic thing. The often-voiced fear that if JFK won the election then the Pope would be running the country reverberated in Grandma's ears. She knew plenty of Catholics, but none were among her circle of friends. Apart from a few specifics of how Catholics practiced their religion, she was hard-pressed to explicate how a Catholic American differed from a Protestant American. But that didn't matter. Grandma had an opinion - or was it a prejudice - that caused her concern and affected her behaviors, but she couldn't or wouldn't justify it.

A year or so after JFK was inaugurated Grandma decided her fears were groundless. After he was assassinated, she believed he was one of the best presidents America ever had. How did she explain that? She didn't. And after MLK was assassinated? Not a word.

* * *

Manny Rosen was the proprietor of Rosen's Fine Clothing for Men and indisputably the finest tailor in town. He was a Jew. Grandma insisted that Grandpa, Junior, Uncle Bob, and I did our fine clothes shopping at Manny's. Our clothes would fit perfectly, be of top quality, and last for many years (assuming we took proper care of them), but they would not be bargains. Jews didn't give anything away. Manny probably still had the first nickel he ever made. They were all about money.

When I got my first job working after school at a Fanny Farmer Candy Shop, Grandma demanded that half of what I earned be put in the bank - and it should remain in the bank. At one point bongo drums attained popularity - benefiting from Harry Belafonte's songs of the Caribbean - and I bought a pair. One day when I was practicing, Grandma asked me how much I paid for them. Then she asked me how often I practiced playing. I admitted not that often. She eyed me sharply and asked if that was a good use of my money. So when Grandma made her comments about Jews being chary with their money, I saw little difference between that and her Yankee tight-fistedness. It all seemed the same to me. Years later, when a Jewess became my wife and the mother of my two sons, and when Grandma came to know and appreciate the remarkable woman she was, the comments about Jews ceased.

* * *

In my Junior year in high school I began dating a girl who had recently broken up with a varsity basketball player. He didn't take the breakup very well. My new girlfriend and I were walking home from a high school dance when her ex-boyfriend stepped out of the shadows to confront me. A scuffle ensued and just when it seemed the situation was about to go beyond the push and shove, a police cruiser pulled up alongside us. We were taken to the police station and given a stern lecture on acceptable behavior. Grandma was called and apprised of the situation and told to come pick me up. When she explained my Grandpa was working and she had no way of doing so, the police said they would take care of that. They picked her up and brought her to the station. She arrived narrow-eyed, glaring, and tight-lipped. She assured the officers there would be no more hooliganism. They piled us both back in the cruiser to be returned home. Not a word passed between us during the trip. Grandma demanded that we be left off around the corner; she didn't want the neighbors to see a police cruiser letting us off in front of our house (somehow disregarding the fact that the police had recently picked her up and brought her to the station). She and I walked the rest of the way home.

Grandma was mortified. No one in the family had ever been arrested before. I pointed out I wasn't arrested, only given a talking to. She said we were not common thugs beating people up. I said I didn't start it and I was only defending myself and nobody beat anybody up. She said I should just have walked away. I said that would just have resulted in my being clobbered from behind. She said I was grounded until further notice. What would the neighbors think? I said the neighbors probably would never know and even if they did, I didn't do anything wrong. She said neighbors always find out. They always think the worst, and "nice" people just didn't get involved in such things. Of course I began to respond to that, but Grandma cut me off, telling me to go to my room. She didn't want to hear any more from me. It occurred to me that Grandma was doing exactly what she accused the neighbors of - thinking the worst and disregarding any exculpatory explanation.

* * *

Grandma disapproved of most of the girls I dated. I often noticed her disapprovals were based not on the girl, but on who the parents were, or rather what they did for a living. I also had a curfew of midnight, unless it was a special occasion. During my senior year in high school I dated Signe, the daughter of a local surgeon. Grandma was ecstatic and suddenly my curfew disappeared. Several times I came home at two or three o'clock in the morning only to have Grandma ask me the next morning if I had a good time. Truth be told, Signe was a delightfully adventuresome girl and Grandma had far more to worry about with her than most of my other girlfriends. However, I chose to never burden her with that particular truth. I figured she had enough on her mind already.

* * *

My grandmother not only had strong opinions as to what did or did not constitute acceptable behavior, who one befriended, or how one's money was managed. She also had opinions on the acceptability of certain neighborhoods and the appearance of a family's abode. Lawns should be mowed, flower beds attended to. Houses should be painted, the yard picked up, trash cans put away. Cars should not be parked on the lawn. Outside toys should be put away unless one was using them (the same went for inside toys). The list went on. Solid, middle class, American values - according to her.

There were a couple of sections of town that Grandma avoided as though they were contaminated with plague. They were characterized by three story wooden tenements with peeling paint. The left and right sides of these tenements had porches on each level that did triple duty as porch, fire escape, and clothesline, the last usually fully festooned with sheets, jeans, underwear, and other sundries. Typically, there was no yard and if there was one it was bare dirt with cars parked higgledy-piggledy with at least one with its hood raised and its jean and T-shirted owner hovering over the engine. No, this was not Grandma's kind of neighborhood.

Grandma's sister, my Great Aunt Dorothy, married rashly, had a child, then divorced in a time in which divorce was infrequent and disprized. She managed to get a job waitressing in a disreputable bar. Child support was not forthcoming and her pay was scant, as were the tips. To the family's shame, Dorothy's daughter, Patty, wound up in the local orphanage and Dorothy, herself, in one of "those" tenements - she couldn't afford anything else.

Grandma made a few trips there at twilight - she didn't want to be seen in the vicinity, never considering that her circle of friends were highly unlikely to be in the neighborhood anyway. She usually brought a bag of food for Great Aunt Dorothy. Grandpa waited in the car. I think he was afraid if he accompanied Grandma, the car wouldn't be there when he returned. After a year or so of these clandestine trips, Grandma persuaded her sister to come live with us. Whether this was more for Dorothy's benefit or Grandma's was irrelevant, both felt better for the move and, I got to know my Great Aunt Dorothy for a while.

It seemed to me that one by one many of my grandmother's opinions was confronted and tested in the crucible of her daily life and they emerged transformed, most often for the better. It also seemed to me that concomitant with her transformed opinions came a softening and a mellowing of attitude that I only wish my grandpa had been able to enjoy before he passed.

THE LEGEND ENDS

This is the way the world ends
Not with a bang but a whimper.
      —T.S. Eliot, "The Hollow Men"

Grandpa and Junior had their differences and as the years ground on and each aged they drew farther apart. Grandpa never fully reconciled to Junior's conscientious objector diatribe vis-à-vis World War II, and he questioned the motives and timing of Junior's marriage to my mother. Junior's enlistment in the Merchant Marines did little to assuage my Grandfather's misgivings. Nor was he pleased when Junior divorced my mother, gave up custody of my sister, and, after hours of wheedling beseechment, not only persuaded Grandma to fund his entrance to college, but to take on the care of me as he pursued a new mate and academia.

Grandpa was even less pleased when Junior left college in his Senior year. I was never told the reason. The subject was *verboten.* And when Junior went from one job to another, Grandpa became disgusted. He, who had spent forty years with the same company as a machine operator, couldn't understand someone who couldn't or wouldn't hold on to a job.

When I completed my third year of elementary school, Grandma and Grandpa told Junior he had neglected his paternal responsibilities long enough. Since he had just married again and was starting a new life, he needed to make me a part of it. One fly in the ointment was that Junior and I had never spent much time together and we were basically strangers. Up to that point I had met him about as often as I had met my Great Aunt Dorothy, usually at Christmas and a few other times during the year. Over my eight short years that wasn't very many times. I had certain expectations, so did he, different ones it turned out. So I spent the next five years with him and his new family. It was a great disappointment on both our parts and when I graduated from the eighth grade, it was decided that it would be best for all concerned if I returned to my grandparent's care. Grandpa was not pleased.

Grandpa worked the second shift and I didn't get to see much of him except on weekends, and the weekends - except for winter - were spent at Camp. As I crept out in the mornings to greet the Great Heron, and as I painted the rowboat, built the patio, helped with road repair and water pipes, and built seawalls, Grandpa watched and weighed and considered. We grew to respect each other and then to love each other. Of course we never put words to this bond, but now and then we would clap the other on the back. He and Grandma began to refer to me as their third son. And as his relationship with Junior faltered and became more distant, so did mine, but for different reasons and from different dynamics.

When I graduated from college, Grandpa and Grandma were pleased and proud. I didn't know if

Junior was proud of me or not - or how he felt about me along any dimension. We seldom had contact. I do know that Grandpa and Grandma were tickled pink with my accomplishment. When I received my Master's degree, Junior came to the ceremony, but left without shaking my hand. My grandfather died before I received my Doctoral degree; Junior was absent, but Grandma was there and she was as puffed up with pride as a blowfish.

Sometime during my sophomore year in college Grandma told Junior to repair our relationship and do something with me. He took me hiking in New Hampshire's White Mountains. I loved it and so joined the Appalachian Mountain Club. Over the next few years, I hiked all forty-six peaks in New Hampshire over 4000 feet - and then the twelve peaks in Maine over 4000 feet - and then the five in Vermont. During that time I branched out into rock climbing and ice climbing. Did Junior ever say, "Good job" or "Well done" or "Let's do some of that together?" He avoided me. When he introduced me to his kayak, I took up white water kayaking, built my own kayaks, had a few great adventures, and published a couple of articles about the sport. Did he say, "Good job" or "Well done" or "How about we do some of that together?" He continued to avoid me. It seemed to me that all my efforts to prove myself to him, to get his approval-his love—only engendered his resentment.

The final straw to Junior's and Grandpa's relationship came when I was about thirty-years old.

He hadn't seen much of his parents, although he called Grandma regularly, and he hadn't been by the Camp for several years running. His absence was glaring during spring cleaning and opening and fall cleaning and closing - those semiannual tasks that we all shared for so many years they had become a tradition. It was far less about the tasks and far more about the family being united, about the small talk, the sharing of oneself with a greater whole. It seemed to us, excluding Grandma because she was still in his loop, that he had turned his back and walked away.

Junior once, perhaps not so jokingly, commented that the ancient custom of primogeniture made a lot of sense to him. Uncle Bob asked what that meant and Junior took great delight in telling him about the first born son's right to inherit all of the deceased father's estate. Uncle Bob became upset, saying that wasn't fair at all and asked Grandma if that was really true. She said she had never heard the term before in all her life, which, while it seemed to reassure Uncle Bob, it never answered the question. Later on, while Grandpa helped Grandma do up the dishes, he was heard to mutter that this primogeniture thing was just asking for trouble. He believed that leaving the camp to all the heirs would be disastrous, as any consensus on its management would be impossible, and no matter who the individual selected, there was bound to be disagreement and hard feelings, but at least that person would get things done. He wanted someone who saw their role as a steward of the property, someone who embraced the idea of a "Family" Camp and was willing to put that concept before personal possessiveness and be willing years later to pass it on to the next worthy candidate. Junior was too self-absorbed and Uncle Bob too malleable.

Grandma and Grandpa changed their will, designating me as the inheritor of the Camp. Predictably, Grandma cautioned me that this was confidential information and I shouldn't tell anyone. Her eyes bored onto mine as she said this. I never uttered a word, not even to my wife (who said later that she wasn't surprised at their decision - nor at my keeping it secret, although the latter wasn't necessary - the last was said a bit snippily).

Nonetheless, somehow, Junior's suspicions became aroused. He paid a visit to Grandpa and confronted him, demanding to know if it was true. Grandpa was deeply offended by Junior's demeanor and reportedly told him he could "damn well wait until [he] was dead to find out." Junior left in a huff and seldom saw Grandpa after that.

* * *

I worked at Dartmouth Medical School and lived in Hanover, New Hampshire. I still went to Camp often on weekends (coincidently it was the same distance from Hanover to Camp as it was from Concord to the Camp) and usually I vacationed there. However, I didn't see my grandparents as frequently as I used to. Grandpa retired from the Rumford Press and waited for Grandma to join him in retirement - in vain. They should have communicated more. She thought retirement would bore her to tears and severely limit what social life she had. She kept working.

I believe Grandpa became terribly lonely, bored, and sad at how his life was ending. He had dreamed of retiring with Grandma to the Camp. He had somehow become oblivious to the innumerable clues, if not flat out statements from Grandma that while she was willing to weekend and vacation at Camp, a full-time dose of it would be absolutely stultifying. She saw Camp as an Augean task to tolerate until they got back to Concord. He sat at the kitchen table, day after day, keeping his own counsel, slowly withering away, until he developed peripheral vascular disease in his legs from years of Camel cigarettes and went to the hospital, where they discovered the lung cancer that the Camels had likely caused as well. He was dead within seven days.

Oh, they could have kept him alive longer, but he had had enough. I remember trying to get him to eat, but he refused, not as a recalcitrant, cantankerous old man, but with his usual grave dignity that brooked no argument. He said, gently, "No, Lad. I've had a full life and now it's time for me to go." And he did.

*   *   *

With Grandpa gone, Junior renewed his interest in the Camp. He began vacationing there again. Grandma went to Camp infrequently. Uncle Bob might take her once during the summer, as did Junior and myself. She went more to spend time with us than for any inherent pleasure in the place. She became the schedule-meister of family time slots at Camp. From the comfort of her overstuffed armchair in Concord, she would designate who would have what weekends and what weeks for vacations.

She returned from one of her Camp visits with Uncle Bob and told me that she learned Mr. Irving, who had been in a nursing home, recently passed away. The news stunned me. While I hadn't seen him the past few years, I assumed that he, like The Old Man of the Mountains in Franconia Notch, would always be there. Little did I know that even that great stone face would fall a few years later.

After Grandpa died, Grandma became preoccupied with the details of her own funeral, and it became her habitude to tell me and my wife whenever we visited where to find her funeral instructions, what dress she wanted to be buried in (it was already cleaned and hung in a plastic bag in her closet), what psalms she wanted sung, where to find her Evening Star necklace to place around her neck (it was pinned to the underside of her jewelry box's top lid), where her obituary was to be found (it had been written a while ago and already had notations to add names of new great-grandchildren), and the funeral home she was to be taken to.

*   *   *

The last decade of life was unkind to Grandma: she had severe osteoporosis in her back and often couldn't get out of bed. She developed weakness in her legs. Consequently, we moved her bedroom from the second floor down to the dining room. Her days of going to Camp - or anywhere else - were over. She became housebound. I tried to persuade her to come live with me, but she refused, saying no one would ever make the trip to visit her, but if she stayed where she was at, least she would see my Uncle Bob, a grandchild, and maybe even a great grandchild every now and then.

I would drive to Concord one night a week, prepare her supper, and spend the evening with her catching up. I'd sleep over in my old bedroom and leave early the next morning to go to work. My wife did the same on a different night. Uncle Bob also helped out. Arrangements were made with Meals on Wheels to pick up the slack. Junior increased his visits to her.

This slow decline lasted for almost a year, until the day Uncle Bob found her trembling in her bed with severe pain. One of her vertebra had cracked while she was rolling over in her sleep. Bob took her to the hospital and, after a while, to a nursing home. No one expected that she would ever return to her own home.

My wife and I drove to Concord one evening to visit Grandma. As we walked through the brightly lit carpeted corridor of the nursing home, we met Junior and Uncle Bob coming out. Uncle Bob appeared awkward, perhaps embarrassed, his eyes looking everywhere except into mine. He mumbled a greeting. Junior seemed in a hurry to leave and didn't want to linger over small talk.

When we walked into Grandma's room, she appeared flustered as well and wouldn't look at me. She directed her conversation to my wife. This was strangely uncomfortable, even weird. I attributed her behavior to her recent difficulty in adjusting to her pain medication. The dose from which she achieved some degree of comfort also made her a bit loopy for a while. After a few more minutes of fumbling at conversation, Grandma asked if I would ask at the Nurse's Station if she could have her next dose of pain meds early as she was beginning to hurt and wanted to go to sleep. While I was gone she beckoned my wife to lean in close, she wanted to tell her something privately. My wife told me later that Grandma whispered, "I've done something terrible…I don't know what I signed, but it's bad…I'm afraid I've done something to hurt Donnie…." (she hadn't called me by that diminutive since I was in middle school.) Then she just stopped talking. When I returned to the room, my wife was coaxing her to say more, but she never spoke or made eye contact with either one of us again. A few weeks later she passed, much as my grandfather had, by gently and firmly refusing to eat.

During those last few weeks of Grandma's life, my wife had occasion to see a palm reader near Brattleboro, Vermont. A girlfriend of hers had just received a reading and it was "amazing." Her friend waxed ecstatic over the experience and urged my wife to go, and she, ever receptive to things spiritual and paranormal, did so. She found it strange that a significant portion of the reading concerned me. She was told that her husband was locked in a chain of father-son conflicts, and that it wouldn't end with my generation. Furthermore, something I dearly loved would be taken from me by my father, but he wouldn't live long to enjoy it. My "second mother" wouldn't live long either. The Palm Reader couldn't or wouldn't be more specific (but ambiguity has ever been the manner of oracles since time immemorial).

*   *   *

A phone call from Junior informed me in a flat voice that Grandma had passed away and asked if I wanted to be a pallbearer. Her funeral was a sad little affair held in the North Congregational Church where she had been a deaconess and her soprano voice had soared to the arched ceiling. But for family, there was hardly anyone there. At age

ninety-six she had outlived all her friends and three
of her doctors - the last a fact she had gleefully
shared more than once with the nursing home staff.
Uncle Bob was red-eyed, grief-struck, and unable to
talk. Junior appeared dour and kept to himself. My
lasting impression of the funeral that Grandma had
long planned for was brief and anticlimactic.

* * *

A week or two later, I received a letter from
Junior. It was brief and to the point. Grandma's will
had been read: Uncle Bob was to have Grandma's
house in Concord, I was to receive a little money,
and Junior inherited the Camp. I hired a lawyer to
check the will, and when it had been drawn up and
signed. Grandma had signed it about four weeks
ago at the nursing home…pieces clicked together in
my mind.

* * *

Late that winter I received another brief letter
from Junior saying the Camp would not be available
for weekends, but if I wanted to vacation there for a
couple weeks, I could, but he expected to be paid a
specified amount to help defray his cost of taxes
and upkeep. When we got there, laden with boats,
books, bikes, and other vacation paraphernalia,
there was a list on the dining room table of
expectations: clean the Camp top to bottom before

leaving, take the garbage with us, no smoking (nobody did anyway), don't touch his kayak, and so on. Since we always did these things as a matter of course, and had for years, it felt insulting. Clearly it was no longer the Family Camp—as it had been for five generations—it was now Junior's rental property.

The following winter I received yet another note from Junior informing me that the Camp wouldn't be available for rental the following summer; he was hoping to sell it. He couldn't afford to keep it. He gave no further details. I heard through the grapevine a few months later that the Camp had been sold.

*　*　*

The following fall the phone rang. It was Junior's second wife telling me that he had just died from pancreatic cancer and that the burial would be in Concord in a few days. My eighteen-year-old son wanted to go; he had never met my father or anyone else from that part of the family. We went and stayed close; there was no sense of connection with anyone there.

About a year later, feeling melancholic and nostalgic and at loose ends, I got in my car and drove to the lake alone. While I wanted to see the old place one last time, I had misgivings. I didn't know what I'd find. I didn't want to talk with the new owners or see any of the changes they might have made. The Camp had always been painted a Yankee barn red; what if they had repainted it a different color? What if they had put sod over the lady slippers? What if they had cut down the giant white pine? I wanted to say goodbye to the Camp as I remembered it, not as a treasure corrupted and altered by change or renovation.

I turned off route 3-A onto the dirt road leading to the gate. It was too early to smell the sweet hay. I passed the Big Frog Pond, turned left and up the hill. The old lightning-blasted pine tree still stood, but its silver-gray, sun-bleached trunk and few remaining skeletal-like branches looked both older and smaller. I drove more slowly along the serpentine dirt road and noticed it had been graded and widened even more since I had last driven over it. I came to the four-way junction and nodded at the massive boulder that we, or mostly Roy, had wrestled off to the side of the road. And then past the Little Frog Pond. There was no Great Heron to be seen, but then it was late morning and long past his breakfast time. I approached the circular driveway to the Camp and peered through the hemlock and young pine branches to see if the yard was devoid of strange cars, ready to back up if it wasn't. My body was tense, breathing shallow. The yard was empty. There were no cars…and there was no Camp - just a naked space leveled by a bulldozer in preparation for new construction. The emptiness was shattering.

The new owners had razed the Camp to the

ground and cleared away the rubble. I stared at the bare scar for a while. It was quiet. No birds sang. The magic had vanished. A few minutes later I drove away.

Made in the USA
Charleston, SC
24 February 2015